The Savvy Gal's Guide to Online Networking (or What Would Jane Austen Do?)

ISBN-13 978-1-60145-253-5
ISBN-10 1-60145-253-5

Printed in the United States of America.

Booklocker.com, Inc.
2007

The Savvy Gal's Guide to Online Networking (or What Would Jane Austen Do?)

By Diane K. Danielson with Lindsey Pollak

Acclaim for *The Savvy Gal's Guide to Online Networking (or What Would Jane Austen Do?)*

"Savvy women need savvy advice, and Danielson and Pollak deliver. The online networking advice in this book is absolutely essential for all businesswomen today. Read it, use it and share it!"
-- Cynthia Good, Editor, Co-Founder PINK magazine

"This book is great! It's smart, savvy, clear, concise and practical while still being energetic, upbeat and fun. It's absolutely chock full of wisdom, tips, suggestions and 'rules' and SOOOO very encouraging at the same time it's supported by data, stats and surveys. There is no better guide into this online whirling world of meeting, networking and building connections."
--Susan RoAne, Author, *How to Work A Room®, The Secrets of SAVVY Networking*

The Savvy Gal's Guide to Online Networking is the book Carrie Bradshaw would have written if she had existed for another few seasons! Diane Danielson and Lindsey Pollak demystify the 'new ways of networking' by offering practical advice about how business women can (and should) use technology to meet new people. In a light-hearted way, the book covers not only what to do, but how to do it. Equally as important, the authors keep reminding the reader that, as in Jane Austen's day, class matters!"
--Carol M. Frohlinger, Esq., Cofounder of Negotiating Women, Inc.

More acclaim for *The Savvy Gal's Guide to Online Networking (or What Would Jane Austen Do?)*

"Reading *The Savvy Gal's Guide to Online Networking* was the most fun I've had reading a 'how-to' book. It's light, yet offers valuable information and tips for improving your networking. As the internet grows into a primary source of communication, this is a MUST READ for anyone in any business."

--Christine Hassler, Life Coach and Author of *Twenty Something, Twenty Everything*

"Networking is an essential skill for all women, and online networking is the way of the future. Danielson and Pollak write in a style that is accessible for all readers, from the tech savvy to the tech challenged. *The Savvy Gal's Guide to Online Networking* explains a lot of the terms we all hear about as well as proper online networking etiquette. A must read for anyone who wants to virtually expand their communities."

--Susan Schiffer Stautberg, President, PartnerCom Corporation

"Highly recommended for anyone looking to stay current in today's online work environment."

--Joanne Gordon, former Contributing Editor for *Forbes* and Author of *Be Happy at Work: 100 Women Who Love Their Jobs, and Why*

Table of Contents

Introduction: Online Networking – What Would Jane Austen Do?

It is a truth universally acknowledged that a woman in search of a fabulous career must be in want of networking opportunities.

Or so Jane Austen would say if she were writing—or, more likely, blogging—today.

In some ways, modern networking is no different than what took place in Jane Austen's novels: it's important to know many different people, attend a myriad of social events, and, above all else, have proper manners at all times.

Yet, today, thanks to the Internet, we now have an entirely new world open to us: online networking, where you can connect with others via a few keystrokes and a click of a mouse. Whether you're looking for clients, funding for your company, a new job, or even a date (you're just as likely to find your Mr. Darcy online as at a formal ball), you can meet or research an infinite number of people through the web. And professional women are discovering that online networking not only opens doors to new business relationships, but it also helps us manage the relationships we already have in an efficient manner that fits our "always on the go" lifestyles.

Just how "always on the go" are women today? And how do women use technology to network? That's something we needed to find out before we started writing a guide for online networking. This is why, in 2006, we surveyed over 1,000 businesswomen from three generations (Generation Y, Generation X, and Baby Boomers)[1] through the *DowntownWomensClub.com 2006 Online Networking Survey: "High Tech or Not High Tech, That is Our Question."* Throughout this book, we'll be using interesting statistics from the survey to illustrate

---

[1] Generation Y (born 1977-1993); Generation X (born 1965-1976); and Baby Boomer (born 1946-1964).

points. Below is the first example, which shows the top six reasons businesswomen network online.

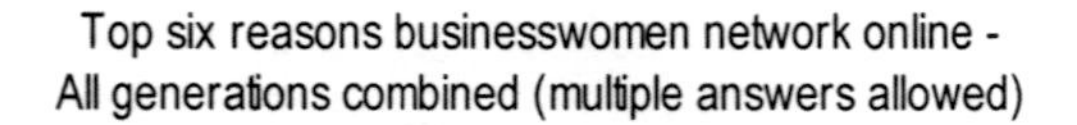

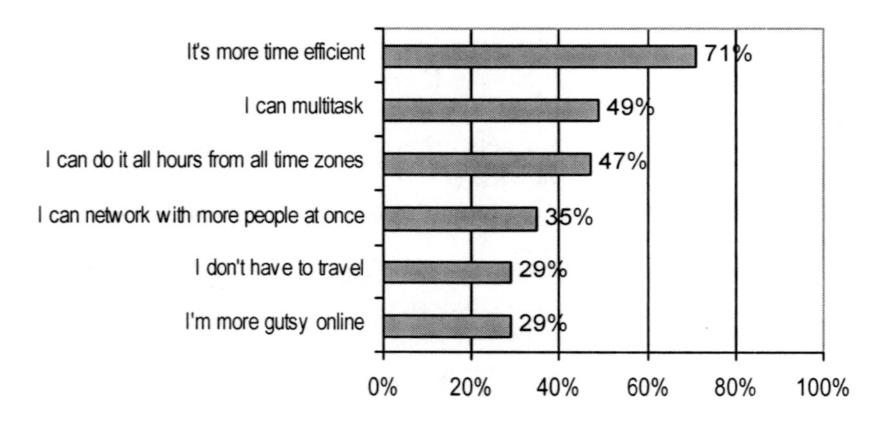

Excerpted from the DowntownWomensClub.com 2006 Online Networking Survey.

As demonstrated by the graph, time management is by far the biggest reason women network online. Yet, even when presented with the timesaving advantages, some people are still uncomfortable and reluctant to participate in the online world. Perhaps the reason is that no one wants to feel like Elizabeth Bennet, fresh in from the country, plopped down and inappropriately dressed at a high-brow event where we're told to mix, mingle, and mind our manners; yet we're not even clear which manners apply.

For online networking-phobes, the Internet can seem too huge, sprawling, anonymous, and, well, *technical*. But our hope is to make it more manageable for the networking neophyte, as well as a realm of opportunity for the experienced networker. So, before we get started, let's agree on a few basic, non-scary facts about how we approach the topic of online networking:

1. **Online networking is not—in no way, nada, not in a million years—a substitute for in-person, eyeball-to-eyeball relationship building.** Online networking complements in-person networking and is most effective when done in combination with live networking. This is why we advocate a "clicks and mix" strategy. In today's increasingly wired society, you can—and should—combine both. For those of you who can't get enough of online networking, don't forget that you need to balance your web interactions with live connections to reap the best results. And, all the face-to-face advocates should consider online networking a tool to help manage and maintain contacts between meetings.

2. **Online networking does not mean that you will turn into a teenager who is attached to a computer 24/7, with 50 instant messaging screens open at once and people gossiping about you on MySpace.com.** In this book, you'll learn how to network online at your own pace, within your own comfort level, and in a professional manner (with other grownups!).

Now that we know what online networking *isn't,* let's talk about what it is.

In this book, we define online networking as any form of relationship building that is enabled by technology. This includes participating in any or all of the following activities that will be explained in much greater detail in the chapters to come:[2]

- Making email introductions—including introducing yourself to a new contact by email and acting as a third party to introduce others by email for networking purposes.
- Using search engines, such as Google, to find information about potential networking connections.

---

[2] One technology we've decided not to cover is instant or text messaging. Both generally occur after a networking relationship has been established (e.g., when running late to that face-to-face networking meeting, we've found texting is a lifesaver).

- Refining your own online presence—first, making sure that you have one, and second, making sure that it represents the professional image you'd like to portray to the world.
- Posting a profile and interacting with other members on a professional networking site, such as DowntownWomensClub.com or LinkedIn.
- Writing, reading, or responding to e-newsletters.
- Writing, reading, or commenting on blogs and message boards.

You probably do a lot of these things already, but may not think of them as networking. Or, some of this might be new to you, and that's fine too. Our goal in writing this book is to serve as a guide for savvy businesswomen ready to add online networking to their always growing skill sets. We hope to explain it all to you in just enough detail so that your eyes don't glaze over, but still provide enough explanation so that you can achieve your own networking goals in the most efficient, effective, and enjoyable way possible.

Etiquette & Netiquette

Before we move on to the fun stuff, we have a few tidbits of networking etiquette that cross all forms of online and in-person networking and that you should keep in mind, no matter where, when, or how you are networking.

- **Give first, ask later**. Nothing is more irksome than meeting or receiving messages from people who talk nonstop about what *they* need and how we can help them. In any networking interaction, it's always best to develop a genuine personal connection first, and then broach the subject of how you and your new contact might help each other. A good rule of thumb: listen more than you talk (or read more than you write).

- **Keep it upbeat and interesting.** Like attracts like, so in the world of networking positive energy attracts positive energy. This is why we encourage people to create unique networking strategies (both online and offline) around activities and people they genuinely enjoy.

- **Deliver what you promise.** Be realistic about what you can offer anyone with whom you network. Do not try to make friends by promising follow-up you may not be able to deliver (such as guaranteeing a meeting with your boss or client). Overpromising and underdelivering is a quick way to lose friends and alienate new contacts.

- **Manage your expectations.** It's unlikely that any one single networking encounter will result in obtaining a new job or new customer. It's best to approach each connection with a specific, more tangible goal in mind, such as securing a second meeting or gaining some valuable insight or information. Consider the networking meeting/email/chat/event a success if you are able to achieve one specific goal.

- **Mind your manners.** You can recover from any faux pas as long as you do it elegantly and with proper etiquette (and a good sense of humor helps too). But, better yet, learn the appropriate etiquette before you act and you'll avoid pulling any faux pas in the first place.

In general, all networking rules boil down to one thing: ***making the other person comfortable.*** When in doubt, put yourself in the other person's hopefully comfortable pumps, loafers, or Birkenstocks, as the case may be. What would you think of your email, newsletter, or blog post if you were in your recipient's shoes? When you're online networking, you can't do wrong when you mentally let your fingers walk over your contact's keyboard!

With many of the same protocols applying to both in-person and online networking, we hope that even the most reluctant networker will find the time and the motivation to get out and meet people, whether it's "clicking" online or "mixing" it up in person.

For those of you who already consider yourselves to be strong networkers, then online networking is even more important to master. Perhaps you have experienced that "tapped out" feeling—that the same people show up at the same events, and you haven't been expanding your list of client prospects or potential new employers? Well, you can *never* feel that way online, where there are infinite ways to meet new people who share your interests. Even if you've found yourself with too many contacts and so little time, technology can help maintain contact in a time-efficient manner.

As we hope to demonstrate in this book, the possibilities open to you for networking online are virtually limitless. And that is something that should make the Jane Austen in all of us more than a little curious and reluctant to be left out, or even worse, left behind.

Chapter 1: In the Beginning, There was Email

We may be stretching it a bit here, claiming that everything began with email, since in the beginning we all know there were cave drawings (precursors of emoticons[3]?). But, flash forward a bit. In Jane Austen's day, people mastered the art of letter writing. Then Alexander Graham Bell invented the telephone and we started chatting away. Many proclaimed that the written word was dead. But, in the 1970s a small group of computer programmers started communicating via electronic mail. Although not widely accepted until the late 1990s, email brought us back to writing letters, only instead of plopping them in the mail, we're sending them instantly around the world at the click of a button.

This is why we can't begin to write a book about online networking without discussing email. Without email, there would be no online networking. As you can see from our survey results on the next page, email is as popular a networking tool these days as the telephone. ***And it's even more popular than the phone for Generations X and Y.***

---

[3] Emoticons are the "smileys" and other expressions used in emails and text messages to convey the tone of the email. For example, ;-) is a wink and a smile. People seem to either love or hate these. We find it helpful in personal emails when we want to ensure that the receiving party understands that we're joking or being sarcastic (two concepts that rely heavily on body language and voice tone and are therefore difficult to convey in an email). But, we recommend you use all three—joking, sarcasm, and emoticons—sparingly (or not at all) in networking emails.

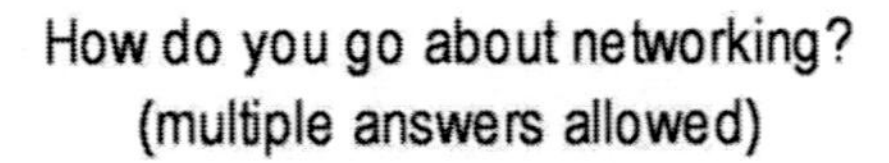

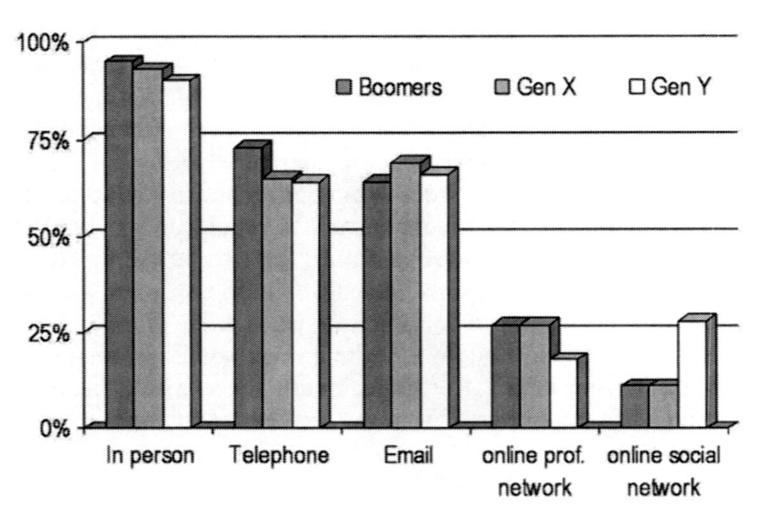

Excerpted from the DowntownWomensClub.com 2006 Online Networking Survey.

The big "E" (email) is by far the most widespread and versatile accessory in your online networking bag of tricks. You can use it to start relationships, build relationships, and even end relationships if you want (although the latter is still somewhat looked down upon in both the personal and professional realm). You can make it very personal, less personal, or completely impersonal. And, best of all for women with active careers and social lives, you can use it 24 hours a day, 7 days a week, from almost anywhere on the planet.

Of course, some people would argue that email hasn't necessarily changed the world of networking for the better. We've all been on the receiving end of annoying spam, rude messages, or other unwanted or unpleasant mail. But these unpleasantries are present in all forms of communication, from telemarketing calls, to used car ads, to middle-of-the-night fax blasts and those darn catalogs that you've never ordered from yet still follow you around no matter where you move. So, we hope you won't let a couple of Viagra ads, unwanted stock picks, or a few instances of poor email etiquette discourage you from getting out there yourself and using email and other technologies to network.

Annoyances aside, we take the position that email *has* changed the world of networking for the better. We love it. Adore it, actually. But we take our email networking very seriously, and apply the same strategy and etiquette that we would apply to any face-to-face networking opportunity—even though much of the time we're often emailing from the comfort of our own homes, wearing our favorite flannel PJs and the occasional anti-aging face mask.

Savvy Tip #1: Know your audience. Are they email or phone people? You never want to force an email person into a phone relationship (or vice versa). We all know that forced relationships never work (despite the fact that some of us like to test that theory every once in a while in our personal lives). However, here are some reasons a person might prefer email to phone:

- **A phone call is done at the caller's convenience; an email can be responded to at the receiver's convenience.**
- **It takes less time to scan an email subject line than it does to listen to voicemail.**
- **Email helps people keep track of communications (much better than Post-it® notes all over the office).**

Jane Austen once wrote, "A person who can write a long letter with ease cannot write ill," which brings us to the most essential piece of advice regarding email networking. If you take nothing else from this book, remember this: ***With regard to any online interaction, never say or do anything online that you wouldn't say or do in person or over the phone.*** Keep that one simple rule in mind and you'll not only network by email with ease, you'll also be much more effective in your efforts.

Savvy Tip #2: If you wouldn't do it in person, don't do it online. This means no skipping over polite chit-chat and heading right to a sales pitch on the first email, or failing to reply to personally addressed emails. The former we call a "verbal brochure," which comes off like an online telemarketer; the latter is an online version of walking away from someone right after she's said hello, stuck out her hand for a shake, and introduced herself. And finally, if you couldn't say something negative while looking a person straight in the eye, then it's not appropriate for email.

Email: The Basics

*Dear readers: When we came up with the concept for this book, we knew we wanted it to be as far from a dry textbook as possible. So, we looked to our heroine, Jane Austen, and created our very own "Austenesque" narrator, a modern-day woman navigating society during a time of great social change. This is how we came up with Wendy, our totally wired executive, who navigates her way through life via the World Wide Web.

> ***Wendy's World, Wednesday, 8:32 a.m.*** *O.K., to-do list item number one for the day—have to find a really good speaker for the company women's lunch next month. What was the name of that woman I met at Carla's party a few weeks ago? She was some sort of motivational speaker or coach or something. I know I got her card...didn't I? Or maybe that was the card I used to write down my number for that cute guy at the car wash? Oh well, no time to worry about it now (or the fact he never bothered to call). I'll have to email Carla and ask her to make an introduction, or at least send me the woman's email address.*

One of the most common ways to network online is to introduce yourself to someone through an email message. You can do this to find new clients or business partners, request an informational interview while job hunting, meet new people in your industry, learn about organizations you're interested in joining, or pretty much any other reason you'd want to form a new professional or personal relationship. Email introductions are simple and remarkably effective. There are two ways to approach this form of online networking:

1. Ask a mutual friend or colleague to make the introduction for you (a great strategy for connecting with high-level people to whom you may not feel comfortable reaching out otherwise).
2. Email the person and introduce yourself.

E-intro Option #1: Introduction through Mutual Acquaintances

When it comes to setting up an email introduction through a mutual friend or colleague, there are several steps to follow to ensure a smooth process:

- First and foremost, make sure the mutual acquaintance really knows the person well. "I once shook Condi's hand at a conference" doesn't qualify someone to make an e-intro. Here's a good rule of thumb: If your contact would comfortably walk up and say hello to the third party at an event and the person would recognize her (and hopefully be glad about it!), then she can comfortably make an email introduction. If this is not the case, an email intro will likely be seen as an intrusion.

- Never assume that your acquaintance will feel comfortable sending an email on your behalf. Simply ask, "Would you feel comfortable introducing me to your friend Bill Gates?" Always remember that you are asking for a favor and your friend or colleague is under no obligation to help out, nor do you want to put your friend in an awkward position. Remember, we want our networking contacts to be comfortable! It's also a good idea not to ask the same person to make too many intros for you—even the most generous and gregarious person can start to feel like your personal secretary if she's constantly sourcing contacts for you.

- Once your friend agrees to make the introduction, provide her with a sentence or two describing what you're doing and why you want to connect. This is particularly important if you're job hunting (if you're trying to leave your current job, you might want to include details about the confidentiality of your endeavor), or if you've just started a new business and your services are still not entirely formed and may require some explanation. Remember that even your best friend or your parents may not know exactly what you do or how to describe it.

  In addition, we recommend you provide all of this information because: 1) it shows that you've given some thought into making this connection and you won't be wasting the time of the new contact; 2) it gives your friend some information to cut and paste into a new email; and 3) your reason may spark another connection idea in the mind of your friend. That's how your networking web grows.

- As is often the case, your friend might just find it easier to simply forward your original email. Therefore, we suggest that you keep this particular email to your friend on-point and professional (i.e., you might want to leave out any cryptic references to the late night antics at your last GNO—girls' night out!).

- Finally, ask your friend to be clear in the e-intro about who will contact whom. This avoids the awkwardness of not knowing if the other person has agreed to connect with you. We generally think it's best for the email to say that you will make the first move if the third party agrees to the "set-up."

Savvy Tip #3: Remember these four basic questions for email introductions: With whom do you want to connect? Why do you want to connect? How would that person like to connect? When would he or she like to connect?

Here's an example of a great email introduction from a mutual friend:

> *Mia,*
>
> *Hi – As I mentioned in my recent email, I'd like to re-introduce you to my friend Wendy. She is involved in chairing a women's affinity group luncheon at her company. She enjoyed meeting you briefly at my get-together last month and wanted to find out more about your motivational speaking.*
>
> *Wendy is cc'd on this email. Let us know if she can contact you directly, and what's the best time and method for reaching you.*
>
> *Thanks so much for your time, and please let me know if there's anything I can ever do for you.*
>
> *Best regards,*
> *Carla*

When you're the introducer (in the above example, Carla), while it might not always be feasible, it's considerate to check first with the individual being contacted in case there is a reason that the new connection might not be welcome at the moment (e.g., the person is heading off for maternity leave, traveling for business, stepping down from the relevant role, dealing with a personal crisis, etc.). However, if you become a trusted referrer, and only put people together where it's a clear win-win to all involved, it's likely that your contacts won't mind your introducing them to new people, no matter how crazy their lives are at the moment.

Ideally, the person (in the above example, Mia) will agree, and then the introducer (Carla) is finished with her job. There's no need to keep cc-ing the original introducer on every message. There is, however, a major requirement on your part to take one more action: Thank the friend who made this introduction for you. It's important to be grateful for any and all networking connections, no matter how informal they may seem. Send your friend an email or drop a note of thanks. Also be sure to check in with this friend by sending another quick email after you ultimately connect with her contact and let her know how it goes. This will ensure that your friend knows you are truly grateful for any assistance, and she will be glad to help you in the future.

Savvy Tip #4: They may not remember when you thank them, but they'll never forget when you don't. You can't possibly overthank someone for making an introduction or sending you some information. In today's often impolite society, a simple "thanks" will make you a standout networker both online and off.

E-intro Option #2: Making Connections on Your Own

Wendy's World, Thursday, 11:55 p.m. *Ugh. Tomorrow's another team meeting and I've done absolutely nothing about prospecting new clients this week. Shoot. I can't sleep anyway, maybe I'll check out some of those networking groups I joined but never have the time to go to. Hmmmm. Here's one that has online member profiles. Let's see if there are any human resource types on there. Hey, here's someone, and what's this? She even went to my alma mater. "Click here to send email." Maybe I'll ask if she's going to next month's alumni event. That makes this sort of a "warm email" doesn't it? A few more of these and at least at the meeting tomorrow I'll be able to say I've started "dialogues" with a few new connections.*

If you're one of those people who just loves cold calling, we applaud you. But, if you're anything like us, you're thrilled that the "cold email" has pretty much replaced the cold phone call. And, when we can search online and find information that turns the cold email into a warm one, sending an email to a new contact isn't scary at all. It seems we're not alone, as in our 2006 DowntownWomensClub.com survey we found that nearly one-third of businesswomen surveyed said they network online because they feel more "gutsy." Probably because rejection by email, or perhaps worse, by the "non-response," is much less hurtful than having someone say "no" to your face (or even your ear).

So, how do you prep yourself for sending an appropriate "warm" or even "cold" email? Put on your gutsy girl hat and realize that you can reach out and "touch" pretty much anyone by emailing them on your own. The trick is to draft an email that is most likely to elicit a response. Below are two strategy suggestions, followed by a step-by-step outline of the elements of an effective networking email.

- **Get your Google on**. Before you cook up an email and hit that send button, first take a few minutes and do some research on the person you're emailing. Google, and other search engines like Ask.com, Yahoo, and Dogpile are a networker's best friend. Use the Internet to find out as much about your potential new contact as possible. You may find a specific connection you share (you worked at the same company, went to the same college, your daughters have the same name, etc.) or you may learn about this person's interests and find a professional connection to mention. You may even discover that the person recently resigned from his position and you'll save yourself the time and effort of emailing! Always do your homework before contacting anyone. You never know what you might learn.

- **Speak in specifics**. Make sure you have a specific reason to contact this person—that you're not just saying hello and asking to chat. Our moms and best friends barely have time to do that with us; what's the likelihood of convincing a complete stranger to simply shoot the breeze with you? However, if you give a specific reason why you're contacting someone, it ups your chances of getting a response. Reasons might include an invitation to introduce your services over lunch or coffee (provided you show some quick relevance in your email), asking for advice on a particular topic, offering a promotional idea for his or her business, etc. People are busy, so be clear about why you are writing this email and why the person should respond.

Savvy Tip #5: Do the one-minute search test before you hit the send button. If you're approaching a new contact via email, take one minute to search his or her name on the web. If there's a wealth of information out there, and it's easily discoverable within 60 seconds, then it's likely that person will assume you have, at a minimum, that base knowledge before you attempted to make contact.

The Anatomy of a Networking Email

"To"

Yes, we're starting with the "To" because before you send that email, you have to have an address. Now this is easy if a contact personally gives you his or her address (on a business card or by other means) or a friend passes it along. But what if you have to go looking for it? That's where the Internet comes in handy. Many company websites have employee email addresses directly listed. Other places to look are through online social networks like LinkedIn or Facebook, which we'll discuss in later chapters.

But, what if a person's email address is not so easily attainable? It's possible the person you're trying to reach is a major CEO or someone who doesn't want to be hit up with a bunch of "cold emails," and keeps his or her email address private. Or he or she may be of a generation that still prefers the telephone.[4] In this case, we recommend you respect this desire to not be directly accessible via a personal email address, and look for a general contact address on the company

---

[4] See our Savvy Tip #1 where you don't want to force a person into either a phone or email relationship. You need to abide by the person's preferences.

website. Usually, info@XYZcompany.com; and then you can send the email with a request that it be forwarded to the appropriate party.

However, what if the person gave you her business card, and horrors, you've either tossed it; left it in the suit pocket that's now at the cleaners; or worse, you handed it to someone else mistaking it for your own? Perhaps you made the assumption that you could easily find the address online to continue your conversation and were surprised to discover the person works for such a huge company that they don't publish all their employees' email addresses on the website (or that there is more than one "Jane" at XYZ company).[5] Even if you're trying to reach someone you haven't ever met before, one trick we use is to see how the company formats other emails on its website, usually: firstname.lastname@xyz.com, or firstinitiallastname@xyz.com. Once you see a standard pattern, you can follow the appropriate format with your target's name and send. In the worst case, it goes to the wrong person (who may then forward it) or it bounces back. But, there's really no harm in trying!

If that doesn't work, we recommend using this nifty invention called the telephone to confirm the appropriate email address. Call the company's receptionist or the person's administrative assistant and ask if the person has a public email address.

"From"

We focus on the "From" line, because your email address says quite a lot about you. In a professional world, you need a professional email address. First impressions, whether accurate or not, are influential and long-lasting. A funny joke between you and your friends (i.e. *YummyMummy@email.com*) might not go over so well with business contacts. The same goes for family emails like *thebarkers@email.com*; not only are they unprofessional, but they also give the impression that other members of the family may have access to that email account.

---

[5] Hopefully your contacts will have read this book (especially the later chapters) and realize that there are steps they can take to make sure they are easily found.

Even free email services such as Yahoo, Hotmail, and AOL signify to people that this is not a serious business email address. However, it's fine to use these for close friends (even if they are business relationships), especially if you have an overly thorough spam filter at work. It's also useful to have one of the free services to use as a backup if your real business email is down or being blocked. This is also smart if you're looking for a new job and you can't use your employer's email to send out resumes and networking notes. In these cases, it's totally appropriate to use a free email service. And, in the case of job hunting, we recommend checking it at home, while not on company time.

As a general rule, people will take you much more seriously when you have a professional domain name (the URL[6] address that comes before the ".com," ".net," ".org," etc.) as part of your email address. It also helps reinforce the name of your company. In fact, many times when we receive a blind email from someone we don't know, we take the email address, e.g., jane.austen@pemberley.com, and go online to check out www.pemberley.com before replying to the email.[7]

If you have your own business, even if it's a part-time gig on the side, invest in a domain name (e.g., janedoe.com or doeindustries.com). Anyone can own a domain name; you don't need to be a registered business to do so. Companies such as www.GoDaddy.com (despite their less than tasteful commercials) offer inexpensive domain names that will even forward messages to your existing account on AOL, Hotmail, etc.

Finally, be sure to set your email account to display a full name in the "From" box. (You can usually set this up through the "Tools" or "Options" function in your email program.) Busy people are more likely to overlook an email from *wb@smarterthanyou.com* than one from "Warren Buffett." We also find it useful when people include

---

[6] "URL" stands for "uniform resource locator." In other words, your online address that comes after the "http://"

[7] In the case of www.Pemberley.com, while we used that name solely as an example, we were not surprised to find the site labeled "Your haven in a world programmed to misunderstand obsession with things Austen."

their phone number in the "From" line, because then we don't even need to open the email to find the correct contact information.

Savvy Tip #6: Make your name memorable. When meeting people for the first time, we find it easier to remember individuals who give us a first and last name. This is why, even though it makes for a longer email address, we like email addresses that include both your name (first or first.last) and the company name. It puts the two names—yours and the company's—literally right in front of our faces. The one exception is if you have a very difficult-to-spell name, then you might want to keep it simple.

"Subject"

Just like a snazzy book title can make us stop and check out a book even if it's on the remainders table, the subject line of an email should aim to do the same. With people getting up to several hundred emails a day, the most they may see is your subject line, so make every word count. This is why you need to be very specific, especially if this is a "cold" or "blind" email, since the person will not likely recognize your name in his or her inbox, having either met you in passing or not at all. Some suggestions:

- If you have a mutual friend/connection and the person gives you permission, use that name directly in the subject line: "Carla recommended I contact you" (but be careful—don't do this without really getting permission!)
- Or, show your mutual connection: "Fellow college alum seeking writing advice."
- Flattery can't hurt: "Fan of your work." (Make sure to identify the work, or it may read like spam to an overzealous spam filter.)

- Avoid generic subject lines: "Networking," "Lunch," "Request," or—eek!—a blank subject line. Many people delete messages with such common subjects, assuming they are spam.

Savvy Tip #7: Choose your subject line carefully. Just as you can't win a point in tennis if you can't even get the ball into play; you can't network effectively if your emails don't get past spam filters and the receiver's delete button. Put succinct details about some connection (however slight) you might have or clearly state your specific request.

"Body of the Email"

If this email is your first contact with someone, make it count! Our rule of thumb is to keep your message pleasant (or, even better, witty, if you can), relevant, and specific. For expertise in this area, we turned to Laura Allen, founder of 15SecondPitch.com. Laura recommends answering these five questions to create a perfect email intro:

1. **Who are you?** Introduce yourself using your first and last name.

2. **What do you do?** Let the person know what you do for a living.

3. **Why are you the best at what you do?** Or, if you're not comfortable saying you're the best, what makes you different or unique? People are more likely to want to help you if they think that you're on your way to the top. But remember, as mentioned previously, we recommend not hitting someone out of the blue with a sales pitch on the first introduction. You wouldn't hit someone up with a sales pitch the first time you meet in person, so don't do it by email. That's not networking—that's advertising!

4. **What can you do to help this person?** Always give something in a networking situation (a compliment, an idea, an offer of help). If

you have nothing specific to offer the other person, simply mention, "I'd be happy to help you in any way I can." Remember to focus on what's in it for the recipient, not what's in it for you.

5. **What's your call to action?** In other words, what would you like this person to do once he or she reads your email? Share information? Meet with you? Chat on the phone? Once you have established a connection and shown your willingness to form a mutually beneficial networking relationship and not just be a "taker," then you can ask for the help/idea/connection/meeting you'd like.

When it comes to "the ask," remember to politely request permission to be in contact with this person: "If you're interested, please let me know a good time to call [or the best way to follow up]." Another good one is: "If this is of interest, may I take you out for coffee to discuss further?" When it comes to sales, we understand that the norm is to suggest a time for your follow-up call (we agree that the burden should be on you for continuing the communication). However, networking is more casual, and it always helps to give the person an option to politely decline.

Remember how we said that we need to make the other person feel comfortable? Think about how you feel when someone makes an assumption that there will be a follow-up phone call as a result of this initial email. Sometimes that can be off-putting. We'd all like to feel we have some choice in the matter when it comes to networking.

Savvy Tip #8: Don't be a networking bully. We know that your product, service, or dynamic personality would brighten anyone's day, and if they can't figure out how, then you would love to explain it to them. However, you can't assume that at the particular moment you sent your email, the other person really wants his or her day brightened by you. This is where networking differs from sales. Your earnest persistence may come off as bullying if you don't leave some "wiggle room" for your contact to politely decline.

"Sign-off"

You'll want to sign off a networking email graciously and professionally. Even though email is a more casual medium than a handwritten letter, you still need a closing. Here are some acceptable choices, depending on your personal style:

- All the best
- Best
- Best regards
- Best wishes
- Kind regards
- Sincerely
- Thank you
- Warm regards
- Warmly

Too-casual closings like "Ciao for now," "xoxo," or "See ya" should definitely be avoided in a business email.

"Signature Line"

Part of the joy of technology is that it makes information easy to find. Part of the pain of technology is that it also makes information easy to lose. How many times have you tossed a stack of business cards into the trash, assuming you can find anyone's contact information online? Make sure that when you send an email to a new contact, you always provide all of your contact information so that the recipient can reach you in the way he or she chooses—by reply email, phone, fax, or horse and buggy. The place to provide this information is the email signature line, where you should include your full name, title, company name, and contact information.

The email signature line can also be a great way to distinguish yourself. You can include a link to your website, the sign-up page for your e-newsletter, your blog, any profiles you've posted on social networking sites, links to buy books you've published, or any other online spots where you'd like to drive traffic.

Some etiquette experts have argued against the elaborate signature line.[8] They claim that it's forcing recipients to read information they don't want. We beg to differ as we often look at people's signature lines, for either the correct contact information or to see if it tells us a little bit more about the person. We sometimes even click on the links in signature lines before responding, especially to new contacts, as it gives us a little better insight into the sender.

As for the complaint about too much information, we feel that since it's at the bottom of the email, it's easily ignored if unwanted. We do recommend that if there are plenty of back and forth emails, you scroll through and delete all but one of your signature lines that may automatically appear. This makes the flow of dialogue easier to read and it prevents oversized emails from being blocked or slow to download (which can happen if you have a graphic in your signature line).

Savvy Tip #9: Always include a signature line or attach a virtual card (vCard—a function available in Microsoft Outlook and other email services[9]) at the bottom of your email messages. Make sure no one has to go digging through their Rolodex™ (if they still have one) to find your phone number. This is also a great way to drive people to your website or other web content you'd like to promote.

Technical note: If you use a picture or logo in your signature line, it may get blocked by certain spam filters. This could mean that

[8] "Email signatures, recipients can suffer from info overload," by Olivia Barker, *USA Today*, February 28, 2007.

[9] On AOL vCards are called "internet address cards."

(1) your graphic does not go through;[10] or (2) your entire message will not be delivered. Sometimes it's best to leave off the image part of the signature line when writing to a new contact for the first time.

To put all of this together, here's a sample email from Laura Allen:

TO: Wendy@AcmeConsulting.com
FROM: Laura Allen
SUBJECT: Carla Goodfriend recommended I contact you – conference workshop

Hello Wendy,

My name is Laura Allen. I'm the co-founder of 15SecondPitch.com. Carla gave me your email address and suggested I contact you. She thought that my 15SecondPitch workshop might be a good fit for one of your company's women's initiative lunches. I've spoken to a number of organizations including: The M.I.T. Women's Alumni Group, Pace University, and the Downtown Women's Club, and I believe my workshop would serve the needs of the women attending your event.

Carla also mentioned that you are a fan of the ballet. One of my clients is a ballet dancer and choreographer who will be performing at the Fancy Dance Theater next Friday. Please let me know if you'd like to attend and I'll arrange to put you on the guest list.
May I call you sometime soon to chat about your conference and how my workshop might be a good fit? Please let me know if there

[10] In this case you want to include "alternative text" if your email program allows it. "Alternative text" is the text that will be displayed in a receiver's email if his or her system blocks your graphic. It's essential to have this if your contact information is included in the graphic (something we don't recommend; it's best to keep graphics to logos, if at all).

is a convenient time to talk for a few minutes. I hope to have the opportunity to speak with you soon.

Best regards,
Laura

Laura Allen
Co-founder, 15SecondPitch.com
Ph: 212-555-1234
Fax: 212-555-4321
www.15secondpitch.com

Follow-up Emails

Woody Allen once said that 80% of success in life comes from just showing up. Well, if that's the case (and it sounds about right), then we believe that the other 20% of success comes from following up—usually by email, of course.

We've all been there: You met someone at an event last week and that hot new prospect's business card is burning a hole in your desk drawer. Is it lame to just write "It was nice to meet you," or "Thanks for being the only other normal human being at that bizarre 60-second-networking-slash-square dance event?"

Not at all. In fact, that's exactly what you should do. When it comes to online networking, it's best to establish a virtual connection as soon as possible after meeting someone in person—even if you don't have an immediate need to meet or speak again. When you meet someone you'd like to keep in touch with, follow up within a week or two while the live meeting is still fresh in everyone's minds. This will make it much easier when you want to connect again for a specific reason in the future.

As you learned in the previous section on emailing new contacts, we love a descriptive subject line. In this case, the easiest and best choice is to refer to the event where you met: "Great to meet you at the Forté Foundation conference" or "Follow-up from Habitat for Humanity fundraiser." This immediately places your email in context for the recipient.

In the body of your follow-up email, you can use the guidelines above for email networking, with two additions:

1. Give the recipient a reminder of exactly who you are—you never know how many conversations that person had, and how many people she met in the past week named Jen. Just give a quick reminder, personal or professional, to jog the person's memory: "I enjoyed our chat about certification programs for career coaches" or "Glad to meet a fellow *Lost* fanatic!"

2. As mentioned above, rather than an immediate call to action, in the case of a follow-up networking email you may just want to say hello and establish a connection: "It was great to meet you and I look forward to keeping in touch in the future. Please let me know how I can support you in the meantime." This shows that you're interested in this person and his or her business and it keeps the door open for future communication.

Wendy's World, Wednesday, 8:55 a.m.

TO: Lucy.Smith@BigCompany.com
FROM: Wendy@AcmeConsulting.com
SUBJECT: Great to meet you in person last night

Lucy,

It was really fun to have someone to chat with at the alumni event last night. Have to admit with the new grads looking younger and younger each year, I can't decide whether those events are reliving my youth or making me feel old. Perhaps we should have a cocktail sometime soon and discuss! Glad I found your online profile last week on that networking group website. And, you're right; it is networking while you sleep, because I woke up this morning to find a reply from another woman I had contacted through the same site. Thanks for being my alumni buddy, and also for the info you gave me about your company. Will forward the work stuff under a separate email!

Looking forward to keeping in touch--

Best regards,

Wendy

Email Networking Dos and Don'ts

Now that you know the basic elements of a networking email, let's make sure your email networking achieves "Best in Inbox" status.

Don't use someone's name if you don't have that person's permission. Ever. Even if it's your mom.

Don't automatically add everyone you meet to your email distribution list. By all means, though, you can send a single copy of an email newsletter or other regular email distribution and ask if they might be interested in receiving future emails. (See Chapter Two for more on e-newsletter networking.)

Do watch your spelling and grammar. Most email programs have spell check functions. Use them. If you're unsure about something, check your email with a grammatically gifted friend. Nothing makes you look less professional than telling an important contact, "Its grate to know they're are other aspiring hula instructers out their." Online, you are what you write, since that's all many people will ever see about you. When someone receives an email or reads an online comment with misspellings, they think one of three things about such people:

Gee, they aren't very well educated are they? Or, hmmmm, they're too lazy to use spell check? Or, worse, maybe I'm just not important enough for them to proofread their emails?

Do quadruple spell check the person's name and company. One of the authors of this book admits that she feels a lot less like networking with someone who doesn't bother to check whether her name is spelled "ey" or "ay." (But, no worries, a sincere or witty apology is always welcome; we, too, make some late night emailing blunders.)

Do watch your tone. Sarcasm in particular does not work at all in email, and you may in fact come across as rude. If you don't know someone, stick to straightforward language and a gracious and polite tone. The same goes for emoticons (those little smiley or frowny faces). Some people like these and some people can't stand them—you never know which side of the fence your new contact is on, so your best bet is to err on the side of caution and leave the smiley faces out of a first email message. In general, if you're not sure an email communication has the right tone or style, send it to a trusted friend first to check it out.

Don't be too "sales-y" on a networking email. Networking is not sales. Besides, nobody likes a pushy salesperson by email any more than they like it in person.

Don't use that annoying red "high importance" flag. Networking with certain people may be urgent to you, but it's probably not urgent to them. And turn off that "return receipt" or "confirm you got this" option, unless it's really vital that the other party confirm.[11] For example, you need to know that a colleague received your email before deadline or if you've been having trouble getting your emails past a

---

[11] This is an email option that notifies you when the other person has received or opened up your email. It usually entails the recipient clicking "yes" or "no" (to notifying the sender) in a pop-up window when the email appears in his or her inbox.

company's spam filters. In other situations, confirmations feel intrusive and add an additional click to that person's day.

Do check your email regularly, including the messages caught in your spam filter. It's a mistake to send a networking message and then not check your inbox for several days. Be responsive. Or, if you must, set your Out-of-Office responder so at least the person is aware that you are not just ignoring his or her reply. With regard to spam filters, it's likely that some completely innocent emails may be caught in them. Before you hit the delete button or the "report all emails as spam" option, make sure all of the messages really are spam.

Do feel comfortable resending an email (once) if you get no response and you feel it's fairly important to you or to the other person. It may be that your first email was picked up by a spam filter or lost in transition while someone may have been out of the office. However, whether it's via phone or email, if someone doesn't respond to two or three queries, it's best to focus your networking efforts elsewhere so you don't gain a reputation as a stalker.

Savvy Tip #10: Think about all the networking emails you get and make note of which ones you answer and why (and which ones you let slip through the crack either consciously or subconsciously). Use this as a reference point for your own email writing.

Email Overload

With more and more people relying on email, it's likely that you'll experience "email overload" at some point in time: whether it's on a daily basis, or on a return from vacation or other extended leave. We confess that we, too, struggle with this and have used the following tips to keep our emails from overwhelming us.

1. **Keep only one "screen-full" of emails in your inbox (i.e., no more than you can view at a glance to your inbox without**

scrolling). Yeah, right (insert sarcasm emoticon here). While we understand the logic of this, and try to act on each email by responding, filing in a folder, or deleting, we can't keep up with the deluge. If you're like us, don't beat yourself up (we don't!). Instead, we recommend setting aside an hour or two on Fridays to go through the past week's worth of emails and respond, file, or delete.

2. **Develop a VIP system**. When an email requires action and you can't resolve it right then and there, create a system that will help remind you that you need to do something. You can move them to a special folder labeled "VIP" or "Action," or use a color-coding system if your email program has one. That way you can quickly scan your emails for the important ones.

3. **Create standard folders**. While these will be unique to your work, we have a few general ones that save us lots of time:

    - Travel (File anything travel-related here, including e-tickets, reservations, frequent flier numbers, etc.)
    - Directions (Save all directions to anywhere here, even the ones you send to other people… it saves lots of time retyping.)
    - Kudos (Anytime a client, your boss, or a friend says something in an email nice about you or your company, include it in this file. Then, before you have a review, or happen to be having a rough day, go through and read them to remind you that you are one savvy business gal!)
    - House, Apartment, or Condo (Include anything related to your home, home repairs, insurance, plumbers, electricians, and so forth).

4. **Write descriptive email headers**. By including as much detail as possible in your header (for example, "Summary of 5.10.07 marketing meeting notes"), you and your colleagues will be able to find the right email quickly.

5. **Use the search function**. Most email programs have "search functions" where they will scan the email for certain words or phrases. This is a quick way to navigate emails, when, like us, you break the "one screen-full" rule.

6. **Have a second email address**. Use this one for e-newsletters and shopping receipts. This is one that you don't have to check on a daily basis and can read at your leisure. If you have friends who circulate funny emails on a regular basis, direct them to this address and then you can read them when you're in the mood for a good laugh.

7. **Turn off your email auto-notice**. When something pops up or sounds an alarm that "you've got mail," it could disrupt your flow of thought and cause you to waste time checking in only to find out someone wants to sell you Viagra cheap, cheap, cheap! Unless you're waiting for an important email, it can wait for you to do hourly check-ins. While it may seem like you're only wasting a few seconds to check each time, the real harm is in the disruption to your concentration.

8. **Avoid vacation overload, part one: preparing to go**. When you go on vacation, you must turn on your automatic reply that you are out of the office. Otherwise, people will expect a response within 24 to 48 hours. Even if you are checking in (and we know some of you will, as we do!), it's best to put everyone on notice that you will only be checking sporadically. One beauty of vacations is that the number of emails you receive often correlates to the number you send, so if you start slowing down your email production the day or two before you go, you'll see them trickle off at the beginning of your vacation.

9. **Avoid vacation overload, part two: returning online**. It's hard to enjoy your vacation if you're dreading the email overload upon your return. One trick we've learned is to put in our Out-of-Office email announcement that we will return on the day *after* we

actually return to the office. You can let your boss and other immediate colleagues know in advance that you really will be back in the office (so you don't get docked an extra vacation day), but it will buy you at least a half-day to respond to all those backed-up emails. When you return, sort the emails by sender, and then answer the most recent ones from the most important sender first. This way you might learn that the most recent email negates earlier ones. And, you can prioritize particular clients or colleagues.

Email is an incredibly powerful networking tool as long as you use it with care. And once you master the art of networking through email, you can benefit from this tool forever...or at least until technology throws us yet another form of communication—mental telepathy, perhaps?

Chapter 2: Spam I Am? The Proper Way to Send E-newsletters

> ***Wendy's World, Tuesday, 10:00 a.m.*** *Oh, bother. Another edition of "A Mia Moment," that e-newsletter from that speaker I contacted about our company luncheon. Sheesh. All I did was ask if she could speak at a lunch group and I get dumped into another email list. The irony is that she couldn't even fit us into her busy schedule. Must be having too many "moments." Oh well, at least she has an unsubscribe button. Too bad, her emails were kind of amusing, and if she did ask me if I wanted to get her newsletter, I would have said yes and sent her my "shopping/newsletter" email address, which I use strictly for that purpose.*

Another important way to communicate, and yes, network, via email is through email newsletters (e-newsletters). This is a particularly good option for business owners and marketers who have a product or service to promote, sales people who want to stay in front of a client, or recruiters looking for prospects. However, anyone with something to say on a topic, or who wants to be considered an expert, can author an e-newsletter.

We find e-newsletters useful for networking for the following reasons:

- It's a way to stay in regular touch with existing contacts.
- It's possible that some of your distribution list will forward your email on to new potential contacts.
- Even if some people delete your e-newsletter without reading it, at least your name/company makes a regular appearance in their inboxes.

Yet, there's one major rule for networking with e-newsletters: ***It's never appropriate to add someone to an e-newsletter distribution list without asking their permission first.*** You always want your newsletter to be "opt-in." This means that someone must opt in, or actively sign up, for your newsletter before it's ever O.K. to add that person to your list. Even if you ask someone in a conversation if they would like to receive your newsletter, and they say, "Sure, just add me to the list;" a far better approach is to send them the information as to how they can sign up for themselves.

Why would people not want to receive your fabulous e-thoughts? Lots of reasons. They may not like to receive information via email, the spam blockers at their company might prevent them, they might have a separate email address where they receive e-newsletters, or the whole situation just puts them in a difficult position if they want to "unsubscribe" and don't want to hurt your feelings. Remember in the introduction when we said that all our networking tips were geared towards making the other person feel comfortable? The same applies to e-newsletter distribution.

These days there are several companies that make it easy to launch your own e-newsletter. Sites like VerticalResponse.com, ConstantContact.com, and MeekaMail.com provide a variety of template designs that you can format yourself, no artistic ability or computer programming knowledge required. Some people do choose to hire a graphic designer or web designer to create their e-newsletters, but note that online templates allow you to use your own logo, font, and color scheme so it can complement your other marketing materials.

Besides helping with the creation of your e-newsletter, these programs also provide you with statistics about who opens your e-newsletter and what links they click on. This can be amazingly useful information, letting you pinpoint which of your networking efforts are most effective and lead to real business opportunities.

Savvy Tip #11: The only beneficial e-newsletter is an opt-in e-newsletter. E-newsletters are a terrific way to build your network, keep in touch with your network, and earn business from your network, but only if people receive them voluntarily. To avoid spam status, ask people to sign up to receive your e-news, and always give them an easy way to unsubscribe. Web-based programs can help you manage this process.

Nancy Loderick, director of network partnerships for the Downtown Women's Club, manages a large opt-in distribution list for this networking group and advises:

> "If it's an e-newsletter that you would like to send someone, I would only send that person ONE newsletter, (forwarded with a personal note from you) and not sign them up to receive the e-newsletter indefinitely. In your email, you might say something like, "Based on our discussion on X date, I thought you might be interested in seeing my newsletter." It's also helpful to explain how the person can subscribe if he or she is interested in receiving the e-newsletter in the future."

Another great piece of information to share with existing and future readers is how often the newsletter runs. Is it once per quarter? Once per week? Even if you have to leave it a bit vague, it helps the individual manage expectations—and fears of inbox overload.

Jennifer Tortorella, an executive search consultant, has a great system for making sure her e-newsletter distribution methods are always inbox appropriate. Here is her advice:

> "At a recent volunteer program committee meeting, I promised to help on a networking event with the Boston Ballet. My job involved handling RSVPs. In tallying the final guest list, I found myself staring at over 100 emails from professionals in the Boston marketplace. I immediately got excited: In my business, new contacts are too tantalizing an opportunity to pass up! I wanted to network with everyone on the list. But, I know that respect is vital in networking, no matter the venue, in order to maintain integrity professionally. Here are some rules I've developed to follow the right online networking etiquette:
>
> **1. Get permission to send your e-newsletter.** Never assume. Ask people, honor the answer, and respond graciously. Also, there is nothing worse than the assumption that because you invited them into your network, you are now in theirs. For example: If I invite

someone to receive my 'Marketplace Update' email and they accept it, there should not be an immediate assumption that I am eager to receive updates about their services or products. (Although, I might be, if they asked!)

2. Always BCC. I send a 'blind carbon copy' email to any distribution list. For the Boston Ballet event, I first sent a BCC email confirming everyone's RSVPs and letting them know I was looking forward to seeing them all at the upcoming event. Then I made a second, separate point in the same email to invite them to become part of my network. Of the 100 plus emails, I received 80 replies of 'yes, please!' Then there were 15 replies of 'Use this email address instead' (preferring personal to professional), and only five saying 'no, thanks.'

In addition, I received this response from one member: 'I do not remember ever getting such a considerate message from anyone. Thank you for setting an excellent example for Internet networking.' Imagine getting that feedback from your network!

**Note that BCC-ing is only necessary when you send e-blasts from your own email address; it is not necessary through e-newsletter programs that distribute individual emails to your list.*

3. Be continually considerate. Touch base with your network once a year and inquire about their continued interest. That courtesy alone is unique and sets you apart. Confirming interest creates a more productive feedback and referral network system."

Savvy Tip #12: When sending emails to a group, always BCC (blind carbon copy) the list. This helps prevent people from (1) accidentally replying to all; and (2) being tempted to co-opt the list for other purposes.

We want to reiterate Jennifer's point about touching base with your list. Not only does contact information and interest level change over time, but reaching out also gives you an opportunity to be more personal.

In a somewhat related example, we know of one former marketing executive who had networked her way into a marketing position where she had little or no experience. Her assistant asked her which reporters were supposed to get which press releases. Not having the foggiest idea, the new marketing VP and her assistant sat down and called every single reporter (this was in the days before email was standard practice) and asked (1) what stories they were looking for; (2) how they would like to receive press releases (by mail, fax, or email); and (3) any important deadlines. While that task was done out of necessity, it was the foundation for some very, very good networking and press relations going forward.

Effective E-newsletters

Now that you have permission for people to receive your e-newsletters, how do you make sure people stay on your list and keep reading? Or, better yet, forward your e-newsletters along to others? During the process of writing this book we made a note of which e-newsletters we read and which ones we don't and came up with these tips to help your next e-newsletters enhance your networking and stay off everyone's spam lists.

- **Keep it relevant to your audience.** In today's oversaturated market, it's better to have fewer "qualified" email recipients, where the likelihood that they will open your e-newsletter and take action is higher.
- **Keep it relevant to your business.** To be most effective, make sure your newsletter relates back to your business and focuses on your specific area of expertise. This helps to build your networking persona as the go-to person in your field.

- **Drive traffic to your blog or website.** Consider e-newsletter articles as "teasers," where your audience has to click on a link to read the full article, buy something, or find more information.[12]
- **Wit, humor, and style go far, at least in getting our attention.** However, without the substance to back it up, you won't get a repeat reader.
- **Make it visually appealing.** Use easy-to-read fonts and toss in a few visuals where appropriate (be careful, however, to not overdo the latter as it could slow down the amount of time it takes your recipient's email service to open the e-newsletter).
- **Provide special offers.** Everyone loves to be an insider, so hook up your subscribers with coupons, exclusive discounts, or early-bird specials.
- **Remember that e-newsletters are not press releases.** Sometimes we receive e-newsletters that simply recount recent business successes of the sender. This is all great, but if they are the focus of a communication, we suggest making it a press release and not an e-newsletter. While you should by all means provide information about your recent accomplishments, make sure that the focus is more on useful information for your readers. Give them some information, tips, or updates of future events that you may be involved in and that may be of interest.
- **Give real news.** Our favorite newsletters are those that give us information we need or information we find just plain interesting. Share some new marketing secrets, a link to a helpful tax-planning article, or highlight a new trend you've discovered in online shopping.

---

[12] Most e-newsletter programs allow you to track which links are clicked on the most, and even see who clicked on them. This is great data to have, because you can do more refined marketing to those individuals who clicked on a certain link, and you can track which links are the most popular with your readers.

We also checked in with Gail Goodman, CEO of Constant Contact, and a leader in the e-newsletter industry who gave us six really good reasons to consider using an e-newsletter marketing service.

1. An e-newsletter marketing service can help smaller companies level the playing field by providing professional templates and automating much of the process.
2. E-newsletter services spend much of their time ensuring that your e-newsletter will get past spam filters (so you don't have to!).
3. Services such as Constant Contact provide tracking mechanisms so you can tell who opened your e-newsletter as well as which links each person clicked on.
4. They include a "forward to a friend" option, making it easy for your recipients to send your e-newsletter along to others.
5. They have automated "unsubscribe" options that comply with anti-spam laws.
6. Through these services you can segment markets and send different e-newsletters to different groups of potential clients or customers.

We agree with Gail that e-newsletter marketing services like Constant Contact are a smart investment. Let someone else worry about the technical details, and spend your time making sure your e-newsletter truly brightens or enlightens someone else's day.

Wendy's World, Friday, 4:00 p.m. *I'm burned out. Time to read my horoscopes for the weekend. Astrology.com doesn't look too promising. Let's check out Tarot.com. Nope. That's not so good either. How about MSN Astrology? Yes. Much better. I can "expect a phone call about a handsome stranger." Well, that would be quite nice now, wouldn't it? Not that I'm really going to sit around and wait for the phone to ring, but a girl does need something to look forward to.*

O.K., now for the non-essential emails. Makeupalley.com weekly update: click, read, delete. Another Pottery Barn update: click, no read, just unsubscribe. (Didn't I do that last week?) Here's another of those "Feng Shui Your Day" e-newsletters from my interior decorator pal. I'm too broke to think about interior decorating. Besides, it would make much more sense to decorate this office, since I spend the majority of my time here. Delete her message, but make mental note to give it a few more weeks to be courteous before unsubscribing. Oh fun! Another issue of "Living an Austen-tatious Life." I know it's weird, but this newsletter feeds my obsession with all things Jane. Besides, it's only four emails a year. Hardly a burden on my inbox.

Here's a sample e-newsletter we created that incorporates many of the above recommendations:

Living an Austen-tatious Life: The Jane Austen Fan Club Quarterly Newsletter

Welcome fellow Jane lovers!

In this issue we're sharing our usual mix of ideas, inspiration, and inside offers for fans of our favorite authoress. To Jane!

MEMBER STORY
***Pride & Prejudice* Production Notes**
By Emma Jones
When I first walked onto the set of *Pride & Prejudice,* I felt like I was walking into the novel I had read so many times. The castles, the landscape, the cobblestone paths…it was every Jane Austen fan's dream. And then, as if things could get any better, I spotted him. Yes, him. Mr. Darcy himself…*read more and view pictures on our website*

OFFICIAL JANE FAN CLUB SURVEY
Emma, Kate, Gwyneth, Anne or Keira: Who's Your Favorite Austen Actress?
Click here to vote now!

SPECIAL OFFER FOR MEMBERS
Discounts on first-edition Austen books!
Click here to shop

Forward this newsletter to a friend
Subscribe
Unsubscribe

For more information about the Jane Austen Fan Club, visit www.livingausten-tatiously.com.

Now, we're not Jane Austen scholars (just fans) and we just put that together off the top of our heads. You can do this too, especially if the e-newsletter pertains to your industry expertise. Even if writing is difficult for you (or too time-consuming), there are services available where you can pull free or syndicated content.[13] However, you will need to credit it accordingly and/or link back to the syndicator.

Savvy Tip #13: Do an e-newsletter review. Go through all the e-newsletters you receive in a month. Make a note of which ones you read and what you liked about them. This will serve as a great outline for launching an e-newsletter that not only boosts your status as an expert, but also makes it past your audience's delete button.

As a final note, you need to manage your expectations. Newsletter lists take time to grow. Remember that it's not the size of your list, but the quality of your list that counts. Also, just because people don't open and actually read some of your newsletters (in fact, sometimes our own mothers are too busy to do so), they still serve a purpose; as often the goal of a newsletter is simply to remind someone of your existence.

---

[13] Sites like www.ideamarketers.com, www.ezinearticles.com, and www.goarticles.com allow you to syndicate others' content.

Chapter 3: Give Better Google

"Everything united in him: good understanding, correct opinions, knowledge of the world and a warm heart"

~ Jane Austen, *Persuasion*

Wouldn't it be great if good old Jane had been talking about us, instead of Mr. Elliot? But let's just imagine she hadn't gone and predeceased us, and instead was alive and well and looking to interview or write about women in the business world. Wouldn't it be nice if she could simply push a few buttons, find our names, and come up with that lovely observation above? Impossible? By dear Jane, yes, as the poor thing left our world long ago. But why shouldn't others, who are fully alive and kicking around the Internet, be able to do a little research online and come up with that same sort of information on us?

Remember back in Chapter One when we recommended that before you contact someone by email, you use a search engine like Google, or equally capable competitors like Yahoo.com, Ask.com, and Dogpile.com, to find out a little more about them? Following the transitive principle of online networking, this means that while you're out there searching for others, you should know (or hope!) that others are out there searching for you.

Now, if you just cringed about the thought of others researching you online because it feels invasive, we hope you keep reading. Having a consistent and accurate online identity is crucial. At the very least, you need to ensure that your correct contact information is available to someone who might find it much easier to type your name into an online search engine, rather than to pull a phone directory out of the recycle bin.

If, however, you don't like the idea of someone researching you online because you're worried about what might be posted on the Internet about you (or by you!), then you also need to keep reading. In this chapter we're going to talk about how to build your professional image online so that it reflects the true you (in your best light, of course).

Thanks to the vast capabilities of Internet search engines, it only takes a few minutes to gather a pretty comprehensive dossier on just about anyone. And, as you know, the more information you have about someone before you meet by phone or in person, the better focused your meeting can be—whether you're looking to close a deal, land a job, forge a networking connection, or even make sure that next date is really as divorced as he claims. A web search can prepare you, intrigue you, or warn you before you waste valuable time and effort.

Now put yourself at someone else's keyboard: How searchable are you? Ignore this question at your peril. We know more than a few people in the business world with the attitude "If someone doesn't exist online, he or she simply doesn't exist."

> ***Wendy's World, Thursday, 4:30 p.m.*** *I can't believe I let my friend, C, set me up on a blind date tonight. Ugh. I hate these, but I vowed to actually make an attempt at a social life this year. And when she called last weekend claiming she had the perfect man for me, I caved. Even though "perfect" in her world means single and breathing.*
>
> *Maybe I can find a picture of him online and avoid having to make eye contact with every guy who walks into the bar. I try very hard to stick to just that basic information when I Google, but sometimes I can't help myself. Isn't info that he made political donations to a right-wing extremist important to know before inviting him out to cocktails with my liberal, "we put the 'L' in left," girlfriends?*
>
> *And while I don't care much about age, as I'm now considered a "mature single" myself, it just starts off on the wrong foot if he tells me he's 46 and I find out he runs half-marathons in the over-50 category. Sometimes it's worrisome that I'm no longer sure what the guy has told me and what I found out for myself. But, my friend, C, assures me that I haven't crossed over the line into stalking. (I'm following them online, after all, not hiding in the bushes outside*

their houses.) Besides, if this was a business meeting, you betcha I'd be Googling!

A person's "searchability" is fast becoming a crucial element of personal and professional reputations. Just as Wendy checks out her blind dates, we're able to check out information about new contacts and potential business relationships. We bet that you've checked out potential employees or clients online, and you can bet that they've checked you out as well. So have conference planners looking for speakers, human resource managers searching for job candidates, organizations seeking board members, and journalists wanting experts to interview.

How Search Engines Work

Ever wondered why a certain page shows up above another page when you run an Internet search? Here's Google's explanation as to how its technology determines search results:

> *[Search results are] ordered by relevance to your query, with the result that Google considers the most relevant listed first...Google assesses relevance by considering over a hundred factors, including how many other pages link to the page, the positions of the search terms within the page, and the proximity of the search terms to one another.*[14]

This means that search results will be higher not just for pages that people click on frequently, but for pages that other websites link to as well. What does this mean for individual people trying to increase the accuracy of a search? It means that lots of factors affect which web pages appear when someone types your name into a search engine. You're most likely to see pages listed for you when:

---

[14] http://www.googleguide.com/results_page.html.

- Your name appears on a website that gets lots of page views[15], such as Amazon.com or a major media outlet.
- Your name appears several times on a particular website (such as your company's site).
- Many other websites link to a site with your name on it. This is why bloggers and others "exchange" links with other people in their network. For bloggers, this usually means that they include a list of reciprocal links (sometimes called a "blogroll") to other blogger's sites on their own blogs.

Search engines employ hundreds of engineers to determine the unique algorithms (or formulas) that determine which sites show up in which order, so it's pretty much impossible to guarantee that a search engine will display one site above another. But, if you're especially interested in increasing your presence on the web or driving more traffic to your website (or away from a site that contains information about you that you'd rather not promote), you can consult an expert in this growing field, which is called "search engine optimization."

Savvy Tip #14: Think of web-searching as a treasure hunt. Start with search engines where you can use a few different combinations of names, including nicknames, or by using "quotation marks" to limit your search to relevant queries. You can also combine the person's name with her company, or even the town where she lives or works. Try the different functions on search engines, such as "news," "images," "blogs," and "groups." Other good sites for finding information about people include LinkedIn, DowntownWomensClub.com, and ZoomInfo. Then there are also blog searches like Technorati and Bloglines.

[15] A page view is a request by your computer to load a single page of an Internet site. This is a more accurate number than "hits" to a website. A single web page is made up of many discreet files and each one is considered a "hit." Therefore, a single page view could equal as many as 25 or more hits.

Will the Real [Your Name Here] Please Stand Up?

Now before you start checking out every ex-boyfriend, take a few minutes and check yourself out, so you can see what clients, colleagues, employers, and even those ex-boyfriends will find when they search for you. You can do this by simply typing your name into your Internet search engine of choice. Although, you may want to try a few, as the results can differ.

Be sure to type in alternate spellings if your name is easily misspelled, or a few distinguishing facts (such as your middle initial, title, company, or alma mater) if you have a common name. You can also try using quotation marks around your name and then adding in your company or town of residence. This may feel weird at first—like you're stalking yourself (and note that this practice is known in some circles as "Ego-Googling" or "Vanity Googling")—but it's crucial to know what the web says about you.

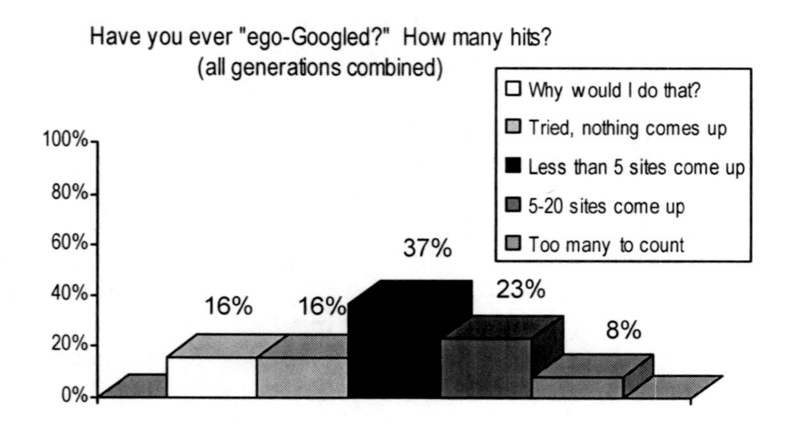

Excerpted from the DowntownWomensClub.com 2006 Online Networking Survey.

Once you've done a search, the next step is to analyze what you found. Hopefully, you found a professional biography with your most up-to-date contact information, and perhaps one or two interesting tidbits. Isn't this what you're hoping to find out about other people? Or did you find an "online twin," i.e., someone who shares your name, but not your life?

Kate Gallivan, a vice president at J.P. Morgan Property Exchange, Inc. searched for herself and found the following:

> "One Kate Gallivan is an activist in New York. The other one is a student athlete at Boston College. I am not at the top on a Google search yet; I'm number four. Although, between being quoted, writing articles, and being active in activities outside of work, I come up more often. I am number one when you do a Yahoo search, though."

Susan Weiner, a financial writer in Massachusetts, shared the following story with us:

> "I was surprised to find I have a lot of 'doubles,' including a former mayor of Savannah, a historian of France, an NBC lawyer, a prominent R.I. donor to Democrats, a nutritionist, the wife of ex-Olympic swimmer Mark Spitz, and more.
>
> Probably the most disconcerting is the New Jersey reporter with my last name. I think our New York City hotel reservations probably got mixed up one time because there's no way I would have requested a 'smoking' room. I actually left her a voicemail over that, but she never called me back."

Savvy Tip #15: Avoid online identity theft. We're not talking about the online theft of your bank account, but someone innocently co-opting your online image. It happens, especially if you have a somewhat common name. The best way to stand out from the crowd is to populate the web with content by, or about, you. You also might consider using a nickname professionally or your middle initial. Both will help distinguish you from any online "twins."

Improve Your Online Persona

All is not lost if your search results are less than impressive, all about someone else, inaccurate, or even if you get that dreaded message, "Your search did not match any documents." The good news is that you can take action. Here are some tips that can help build your web presence, depending on your company's policies, your professional ambitions, and your comfort with the Internet:

1. If possible, make sure your most current professional bio appears on your company's website. This is where most people will expect to find information about you. Next, check the websites of any nonprofits or other organization where you volunteer or have a board position to see if they identify you correctly. If you don't already do nonprofit work, here's another reason to start!

2. If you find any errors or content that's less than impressive (or inaccurate) on someone else's site (for example, a disgruntled colleague mentions you in her "IHateMyJob" blog), send a note to the blogger or webmaster of the offending site and request a correction or deletion. Media websites aren't likely to make a change, but most other organizations should agree to fix any incorrect or misleading information. If there's no way to change content, your best course of action is to add more positive content about yourself online, to "cover up" the negative stuff.

3. Create a profile on a professional networking site, such as LinkedIn.com, Ryze.com, Spoke.com, or a niche site like DowntownWomensClub.com's DWC Plus member directory. Many of these sites will allow you to make your profile viewable by the public (which means it will be identified by search engines). These online profiles include plenty of space for you to post information about your current position, previous positions, schools attended, organization memberships, and more. You'll find much more information about such sites in the next chapter.

4. Get published on the web.

    - Write for your company or organization's newsletter. They often publish these online, and they're always looking for content.
    - If you belong to a professional association, and particularly if you serve on a committee or hold a leadership position, offer to write a short online article on a topic related to your expertise. Likewise, if you've spoken at an industry event recently, ask if excerpts from your remarks can be archived on the host organization's website.
    - You can pitch articles to online magazines such as www.sbtechnologymagazine.org, www.bluesuitmom.com, or www.womenentrepreneur.com.
    - You can post articles on community blogs such as www.gather.com, www.helium.com, or www.workitmom.com or simply write articles for your own website if you have one.
    - You can also "syndicate" articles, i.e., post them to a site which promotes your articles to other authors of blogs, websites, and e-newsletters, who can pick up your content to run on their sites, provided they include the proper credit with links back to your own site. Sites that provide this service include www.ideamarketers.com, www.ezinearticles.com, and www.goarticles.com.

5. Review books on www.Amazon.com, www.BarnesandNoble.com, or send your review to a blog related to your industry. Note that for maximum exposure you should register to post your reviews with your real name, not a username like "SalesBookGuru" or "NewJerseyHRWoman."

6. Of course, if you're really interested in building your web presence, start blogging. We'll have more about that in later chapters. But, if your goal is to improve your visibility as an expert in your field and you like to write, this is a great strategy.

7. Try running a search of some professionals you admire and see where *they* show up online. Perhaps you can contribute to some of the same websites or register for the same directories or virtual communities.

8. Include links to your favorite pages or online profiles in your email signature line. This will drive more eyes to the online items you like and will push those pages toward the top of any search engine results.

Online Press Releases

Press releases are the traditional way to attract media attention in the offline world, and they've easily transitioned to the world of the web. Although on the Internet, they aren't just about pitching stories to the media. Posting announcements about your business or professional accomplishments is another great way to improve your online searchability. You can post your press releases for free or extremely low cost at several services, including PRweb.com, PRFree.com, and PressRelease365.com, where they'll get picked up by search engines, blogs, and even news organizations.

Savvy Tip #16: Be your own online PR agent. Did you join a new firm, get a promotion, or close a major deal? Don't forget to let the online world know about it. Submit your news to your college alumni magazine, local newspaper, or trade organization. Many of these publications also run the announcement online, which means it will be picked up by search engines if people are looking for the latest information on you.

Kirsten Osolind, CEO of RE:INVENTION Marketing, a marketing and PR firm that helps companies market to working women, emphasizes the importance of submitting press releases to help you build your online image. She gives us some interesting statistics:

> "A small investment in press release distribution can attract thousands of visitors who would never otherwise hear about you or your website. By posting press releases online, you're not only reaching the media through the network, wire service, news portals, and syndicated sites, but you're also reaching anyone who searches for your name or for a relevant topic on major search engines such as Google, Yahoo, and MSN. Here are some stats to consider:
>
> - 98% of journalists go online daily
> - 92% to conduct article research
> - 81% to use search engines
> - 76% to find new sources of experts
> - 73% to find press releases"

Remember, if journalists are finding you through an online press release, then other people are too. This is why we are categorizing press releases as a networking tool and why you should consider the occasional press release as a strong networking strategy.

You don't need an expensive PR firm to do basic press releases. When you do something newsworthy—such as winning an industry award, receiving a notable promotion, acquiring a new client, joining the board of a nonprofit, donating a significant amount of money or products to charity—write a press release about it (most online services have a form to fill in), or make sure your company's marketing or communications department does so. Try to give your releases a relevant headline, and integrate keywords related to your career or business (so that anyone searching for such words will also find your press release) and include a call to action and contact information (phone number, email address, and/or website address).

Here are three tips to writing an online press release that we always abide by:

- Do not bury the lead. People have much shorter attention spans online than they do in print. You need to put the hook in the first sentence.
- The first five words of your headline are the most important. This is because many online press releases run as RSS feeds.[16]
- Tie in relevant trends and stories. Whatever the hot story is, if you can include a popular and newsworthy term or keyword, people searching for that topic may find your press release. For example, if you just conducted a study on the number of young people voting in local elections, and you can compare it to the number of votes on a typical week on "American Idol," you'll get the attention of people who are looking for American Idol news. However, use this tip cautiously because it only really helps you if the types of people searching for reality show gossip are also your target market.

Savvy Tip #17: Assume your audience suffers from OADD (Online Attention Deficit Disorder). When writing an online press release, craft a headline that will catch people's attention in the first five words. Then, make any important information easy to find and include links back to your site for more detailed information. Don't try to do too much with a single press release. It's better to run a few back to back, rather than fit it all into a single release.

Once your press release is posted online, it begins to accrue a search engine ranking and will show up on people's computer screens if they search for your name, your company, or the keywords you've included in your release. Any press release you post on the Internet will remain

[16] RSS stands for Really Simple Syndication. This is where a service such as a homepage or blog pulls together headlines and sometimes the first few sentences of a group of news items. For example, if you have a "My Yahoo" homepage, you might be getting Reuters or Associated Press headlines on your homepage. Most RSS feeds only have enough space to run the first few words of a headline.

visible online for an unlimited amount of time. Of course, as more recent news begins to accumulate over the next few weeks and months, the press release will begin to naturally move down in the search engine rankings, and therefore may not be as easily found. Remember to post a copy of any release on your own personal website, if you have one, for additional exposure to eager eyeballs.

What's the benefit of all this attention? Posting press releases increases your online image in a professional, trustworthy way, which in turn:

- proves your legitimacy in the business community—when people check you out online before meeting with you or returning a phone call from you;
- attracts the eyes of recruiters and hiring managers (see Chapter Six);
- results in new links to your website, or any website you include in your press releases;
- garners potential media attention, adding to your online persona; and
- builds your brand quickly and extensively.

Savvy Tip #18: Build your online portfolio. The more information you post online about yourself, the more you control what people find when they type your name into a search engine. Press releases in particular are a relatively easy and accepted way to disseminate information that will drive networking opportunities your way. Depending on your goals, online content can attract media attention, potential clients, headhunters, conference speaker coordinators, or anyone you hope will find you online. Always remember that networking, online or offline, is not just about who you know; it's about who knows "what" about you.

Pictures that Pop!

Wendy's World, Saturday, 9:30 a.m. *Surprisingly, Thursday night's blind date wasn't absolutely awful. No love at first sight, "Sleepless in Seattle-worthy," fireworks-shooting-off-over-our-heads moments, unfortunately. But, he was quite funny and a true gentleman, even after we determined that I should not be allowed near sharp objects like darts after a glass or two of Chardonnay. (I do so hope that barkeep's arm heals quickly.) All in all, BD (Blind Date) guy seemed fairly well adjusted for a 40-something "never married" (a species of male who more often than not, has more issues than a DWK, i.e., divorced with kids).*

The bonus is that he may be a great business contact. He actually seemed somewhat interested in my consulting work. Will definitely keep him in the rotation. Not that there's anyone to rotate him with, but that's not the point, is it? However, it did make me a bit nervous when he made comments about what HE found about me online. I guess I better do some ego-Googling.

Egad! How did that God-awful picture from my last company's webpage stay up there? Have no idea, but at least I should counteract it with a better one somewhere. Hmmmm. Let me check out that women's business website that I used to contact those HR reps last week and see (1) if there are any photographers on there (it's always nice to give another gal some business); and (2) if there are any women whose professional photos I like. I could just jot off an email and ask who took the photo if they're local. (Actually, that's not a bad way to start chatting.) Then I could post a profile with a photo that doesn't scream "early 1990s;" no need to flaunt my age—it's hard enough to get dates as it is.

When it came time for us to write about online images, we couldn't help but hear the old Madonna song, *Vogue*, running in our heads. Now, Madonna may fashion herself a modern-day Jane Austen, what with her faux English accent and lifestyle. However, when it comes to inventing an image, she knows what she's talking about. The beauty of the Internet is that even those of us who are not followed around by our own personal stylist can still be a "lady with attitude" and strike a professional pose. Online appearances are a large part of your image, because it's not just your name that people can find online, it's also your face. And that can be a good thing.

In our DowntownWomensClub.com survey, when we asked businesswomen why they didn't network online, the top two reasons were "too impersonal" and "can't leverage personality and image." We aren't buying those excuses! Perhaps these women just weren't trying. There's nothing like a smiling photo to make a personal connection.

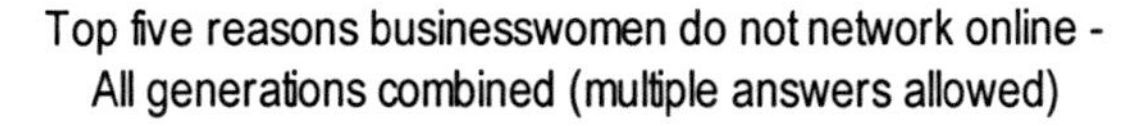

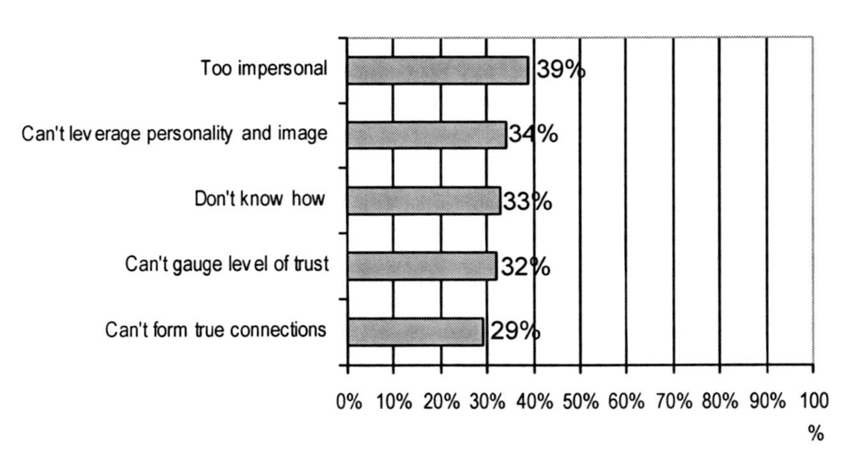

Excerpted from the DowntownWomensClub.com 2006 Online Networking Survey.

Many websites, such as the DowntownWomensClub.com's DWC Plus member directory, allow you to post a photo along with the text you supply. We all know that a picture is worth a thousand words, and it can also be worth a thousand clicks…if you use the right kind of photo. For tips on taking and choosing the best image, we checked in with photographer Nancy Carmichael of Onyx Productions in Winthrop, Massachusetts. She advises:

- Have your hair done the day of the shoot. Nothing looks better than a good blowout.
- Don't forget a manicure, as sometimes your hands may be in the shot.
- If you wear makeup, either have the photographer book a makeup artist or consult one yourself. Makeup needs to be a little heavier for the lights.
- Avoid turtleneck or high collar necklines because they make you look restrained and uptight.
- Don't wear stripes or plaids. They look especially busy on computer screens.
- If you're having a bad day you should probably reschedule. The camera picks up everything!

Just for fun, we went through a couple of websites with online photos and came up with a few of our own suggestions for "pictures that pop!"

- **Check the trends at the door.** Yes, the eighties are back when it comes to fashion, but they likely won't be back again for another 20 years. Jewelry and accessories are big "time-stamps," so unless it's a true classic that you've worn year after year for more than a decade, leave that plastic fuchsia flower pendant in your jewelry box.

- **Sex sells, but hopefully that's not what you want to advertise on the web.** We love glamour shots. After all, why should our professional photos be stuffy if we're not? But if it crosses the line into too sexy, it's time to button up a bit. Not sure where the line between sexy and powerful is? Ask a few male friends. Believe me, they'll tell you.

- **Show some face.** Online pictures are small, so make sure your lovely mug is up front and central. In fact, some of the pictures we liked best were cropped close to the face and didn't even contain the person's whole head.

- **Smile.** Whether it's with your mouth or your eyes, lighten up. Who wants to network with Ms. Grumpypants?

- **Color your world.** Bright colors are eye-catching, but be careful. They should pop, not overpower. However, if the focus is on your face as mentioned above, even the brightest colored clothing shouldn't detract.

- **Get your pixels in the right proportion.** Learn how to publish your photos on the web. Most websites can only publish jpegs or tiffs, which means photos which end in the letters .jpg, .tif, or .gif. They also need them in a smaller resolution than a print piece would need. This means 100 dpi (dots per inch) for online photos; 300 dpi for print photos; and a smaller file size, less than 3.5 MB (megabytes), for online photos. Why is smaller better in this case? Because it's all about the download time. The bigger the file, the longer it takes to download. If all this is completely foreign to you, ask the photographer to give you two types of digital photos—one for print and one for online.

Finally, remember that you've got to stay diligent about online content and posted photos. Just like the web itself, your online image is a never-ending work in progress and content stays up until you remove it. While you don't have to monitor your online identity minute-to-minute as many companies do, you should check in on your virtual self regularly. This is particularly important when you're undertaking a job search or slated to speak at a conference (or even going on a date!), when others are more likely to be checking you out online.

Savvy Tip #19: Stay alert. One easy way to keep track of your online image is to set up a news alert. This is a service offered by almost all search engines where you can type in your name (or your company's name) and whenever you're mentioned on the Internet, the search engine will send an email with a link to the site. Check out Google or Yahoo for free offerings.

Chapter 4: Social Networks – Classmates and Friendster and MySpace, Oh My!

Ever play the game Six Degrees of Kevin Bacon? That's where you try to link any actor to Kevin Bacon through the movies he or she starred in. For example, *Pride & Prejudice* star Keira Knightley was in *Love, Actually* with Emma Thompson, who starred in *Sense & Sensibility* with Hugh Grant, who shared the screen with Colin Firth in *Bridget Jones' Diary*. And Colin? Years ago he wowed us all as the original "Mr. Darcy," but more recently he made a movie called *Where the Truth Lies*, with, you guessed it, Kevin Bacon.

Why Kevin Bacon? We're not sure why he's so central, but there are theories out there that everyone in the world can be connected to everyone else through a chain of six people. This is really what "social networking" is all about—finding or making connections and linking people together.

Some of us have heard of social network analysis in reference to tracking down terrorists; or we may have experienced it in the workplace where really expensive management consultants fly in to spend time at your company following you and your colleagues around all day to see who you talk to. The theory is that the people you talk to (your social networks) will provide clues as to how information is disseminated within an organization or who are the key influencers in the office—as well as more important revelations, like who hovers around the kitchen after meetings to ensure they always get first dibs on the best leftover meeting sandwiches.

Online "social networks" are about linking people to each other and disseminating information. However, "social networks" in this online networking context are the proactive communities formed by the online participants themselves.

This leaves the big question for everyone over the age of 35, including Stan, the guy who's munching away on that stale, leftover meeting sandwich: Why would I want to be part of a social network?

To teenagers and most twenty-somethings, that question is like asking "Why would you want to have friends?" Putting aside all the sinister proclivities that might exist, MySpace and comparable social networks are a way to find others with similar interests and make friends beyond your geographic limitations. For high school and college students, it's another way to form a fan club, meet a pen pal, get people to sign your yearbook, and even put on a much more popular persona. Remember how much fun it was to have camp and pen pals who would blindly accept the embellished versions of your life and never know of the day-to-day, not-so-cool parts? Imagine putting that out there for the whole world. Even for those of us a bit older, it's a way to stay in touch with friends and to check out the skinny on "new friends" (hopefully including that cute guy you met at the bar).

In this chapter, we look at some of the less business-oriented social networks, because they are leading the industry in innovation and popularity and have had an enormous impact on society. They are also influencing how younger generations network, as evidenced by the chart below. For those of you who, like us, still remember vinyl LP records and rotary phones, these online networks are where your youngest employees, your future employees, your Gen Y customers, and many people you'll want to network with in the future are networking today. Ignore this trend and you might be put out to pasture a bit earlier than expected!

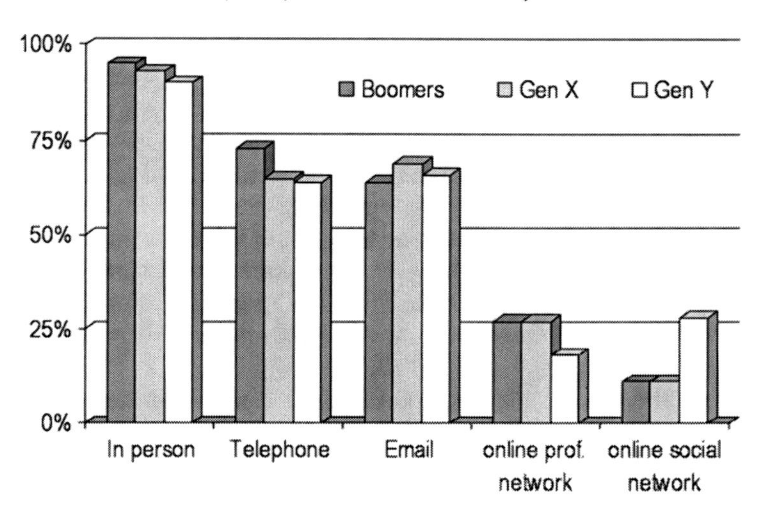

Excerpted from the DowntownWomensClub.com 2006 Online Networking Survey.

See You at the Reunion

Wendy's World, Thursday, 8:18 p.m. *Shoot, it's Thursday and I haven't done a darn thing to help M with our class reunion. Not sure how M even roped me into this; I haven't been home for years. But, she's married to her high school sweetheart, has four kids, lives in the same zip code, and wants to relive her glory days. If she wasn't my best friend from childhood, I'd probably hate her guts. "Oh, but Wendy," she always says. "You have such a glamorous life, dating in the big city and traveling around the country." Yeah, I just spent last month at a client site in Poughkeepsie and now I'm sitting all by my single self in my single gal's apartment eating supermarket sushi and sipping "Two Buck Chuck" Chardonnay from Trader Joe's. But, what the heck, let's get online and start*

> *trying to track down people; maybe somebody actually got interesting. First stop, Classmates.com.*

In the *DowntownWomensClub.com 2006 Online Networking Survey: High Tech or Not High Tech, That is Our Question,* Classmates.com was used by 44% of members surveyed, followed by LinkedIn.com at 39%, and MySpace and Friendster were tied at 19% each. Why is Classmates.com so popular? That's easy—it's all about the reunions. If you try to organize a class reunion in the near future, your first stop should be registering both your information and the reunion information on Classmates.com and other reunion-oriented sites. Then you can see who else is registered and start connecting. Even if you don't have a reunion, it's still great fun to check out your former classmates. You never know who you might want to reconnect with.

There are other websites dedicated to finding former classmates, including Reunion.com, and for recent graduates, Facebook.com. While the business leader in social networks, LinkedIn.com (which we'll discuss in detail in the next chapter), does not prompt members to list where they went to high school, it does include a function that allows you to find college and graduate school classmates who have listed their alma maters in their profiles.

Savvy Tip #20: If planning a high school or college reunion, it's best to check and register on as many alumni-oriented sites as possible (including your own former high school site—many have options to do so). Some require a small registration fee, but think of how much you can save in postage by doing the invites by email, not to mention building a new database of potential business contacts.

Will You Be My Friend?

We were probably three or four years old when we first asked someone if they would be our "friend." And it was probably directed at the kid in the sandbox who was using the red shovel that we really wanted to play with at that moment. But, since that time in the sandbox, a whole new industry about making friends has developed.

One of the pioneers in this "social networking" industry is appropriately named Friendster.com. While losing ground to MySpace in recent years, it's still a viable social network and popular with the under-35 crowd. Basically, like most social networks, you register for free and post a profile, not unlike one you would post on a dating site. You can sign up on your own, or you may receive an email invitation from a friend, asking you both to join and to be part of his or her network.

Then what do you do? Well, that's a very good question. You'll start by filling out personal information, ranging from your age to your favorite movies to what kind of people you want to meet and why (friendship or dating). Social networking sites also encourage you to upload several photos to accompany your profile. It's definitely tempting to post lots of funny, quirky, maybe even sexy snapshots since these sites are so fun and casual. But even if you don't ever plan to use your Friendster, Facebook, or MySpace profile for any of your professional networking, remember that people can still find you here. So be careful not to post any images you wouldn't want a professional contact to see. You don't have to follow all of the professional photo tips from Chapter Three, but keep in mind their overall message: image counts. Think of social networking websites as if they were company picnics or cocktail parties; it's O.K. to have fun and show your lighter side, but you don't want to be the one with a lampshade on your head.

Some people keep their friends updated on their lives via Friendster. Some just use it as a way for others to find them. There are some businesses and alumni groups who make use of Friendster, but generally, they cater to younger audiences. Still, we've heard stories about one "friend" who only learned that her boyfriend was breaking up with her because he changed his profile on Friendster from "in a relationship" to "single."

Basically, if you join a social network like Friendster, you can do one of four things:

1. contact others you know who are already on there (perhaps you joined in response to one of their invitations);
2. search for "friends" you already know by name, keyword, school, or company;
3. peruse the networks of your existing "friends" for people you want to meet; or
4. sit back and wait for others to contact you.

Like Wendy, when faced with an upcoming college reunion and being consummate networkers, we made attempts to locate "friends" on a few reunion websites who might have gone to high school or college with us. We tried Friendster ourselves and found that there were only a handful, if any, in the over-35 age group; but as you go younger (around 30 years old), the numbers increased dramatically.

MySpace Cowboys: Welcome to the Wild, Wild West

I'm not sure anyone can exist today without hearing about MySpace, the "bad boy" online network launched in 2003 that is generating the most publicity, both good and bad, as well as the most web traffic.[17] While it's generally not used for business networking, we include MySpace here because it's important to understand why the site is so popular and what this might mean to the workplace going forward.

For those who are new to the world of online social networks, you're probably thinking of Internet chat rooms where you can go in and start writing to random people who are all visiting the same room or webpage, à la Meg Ryan and Tom Hanks in *You've Got Mail*. Well,

[17] Alexa Web Search (www.Alexa.com) ranks MySpace in the top ten most trafficked sites behind Yahoo, MSN, Google, YouTube, and Windows Live.

the world has changed since 1998 and MySpace and other next generation social networks operate differently.

Once you register for MySpace, like on Friendster, you're given your own personal webpage to fill in with information about who you are, your interests, and what you might be looking for in "friends." If you're thinking this sounds a lot like online dating sites, you are quite correct. In fact, on one of the author's forays onto MySpace in the name of research, the only "friends" who found her page were young men sending in "beefcake" photos. While flattering, these "friends" were not particularly helpful for business.

However, should the shirtless male pictures not discourage you from venturing on to find people with like interests in music, movies, and other items of intrigue (or to check up on what your child may be doing), you can pick out a username, post your profile, post pictures, music, or blog entries[18] on your page. You can then invite others to visit your page or just sit back and see who wants to become your "friend."

In case we still haven't sold you on why millions, actually, hundreds of millions of people are flocking to MySpace, this is akin to keeping a diary (albeit public, not private); forming cliques online (the "Top Friends" option allows individuals to rank their friends); decorating your room with posters of your favorite stars (now they're decorating web pages); starting a fan club (music and video sharing); and chatting for hours online with best friends they saw in school less than an hour ago. All of these behaviors are typical teenage pastimes; it's the technology that makes them so different.

For those of us a bit older, online social networks are a way to communicate with others who share our interests, and develop relationships online that defy geography and often demographics. It also allows members to reinvent their images online. Thus, MySpace and other social networks like Youtube.com have spawned "celebrities" who are the reality stars of the Internet. Perhaps you've heard about Lonelygirl15 or "The Bus Uncle." As our heroine, Jane Austen, would

---

[18] See Chapter Seven re: blogs.

say, "One half of the world cannot understand the pleasures of the other."

Why do we refer to MySpace as the Wild, Wild West? Because it's millions of people in a community all vying for attention with no set rules, or a way to enforce what rules might exist. It's a new territory that will eventually sort itself out, but before that happens, it's anything goes. And, while companies targeting the youth market are putting up MySpace pages (and checking out the site may help you understand your younger employees), we've yet to find it useful for business networking.[19]

Savvy Tip #21: MySpace ignorance can hurt your child. If you have a child 14 or older, you need to register for MySpace (which is free) and check to see if your child has a webpage up there. Not only will you be able to monitor whether it is safe from online predators, but if you take a constructive approach, you also will be able to share an experience with your child as well as learn a little bit more about technology.

Savvy Tip #22: MySpace ignorance can hurt your career. If you are a recent graduate or twentysomething, it's possible that your MySpace page could hurt your job prospects. Yes, employers are on there (especially the ones who have kids!).

- **There are privacy settings for profiles: learn them and use them.**
- **Avoid guilt by association. While you might have appropriate images or content, monitor your friends' pictures and comments that appear on your page, or if they "tag" (i.e. caption) a risqué photo on their own page with your name.**

---

[19] Although we did find that dear old Jane Austen herself seems to have emerged from her grave and created her own MySpace page at: http://www.myspace.com/iamtherealjane.

- **Demonstrate that you know the difference between personal websites and professional websites by having a professional online profile that the employers can easily find (more details in the next chapter).**

Chapter 5: Social Networking Grows Up

Wendy's World, Friday, 11:15 p.m. *Back from second date with BD (Blind Date) guy. He's really nice, and we do just babble on like I do with my girlfriends. But, he's just no Chris Martin, who was, of course, my high school crush and has been the comparison for every man I've ever met. Speaking of Chris, I couldn't find him on Classmates. Maybe I'll try LinkedIn. I think I remember him getting a football scholarship to State...*

Oh my god, omigod, omigod, it's him, it's got to be him. Right age, right college. He's in sales. Figures, with his looks. No picture, bummer. I'll try a few other industry-related networks. Maybe he doesn't know about the reunion? He wasn't on M's official list. I guess I could send him a LinkedIn invitation to connect. But, no, it's Friday night, he'll think I'm a total dweeb (or worse, not have any clue who I am). I'll just wait until tomorrow or something, and say that I was spending the weekend helping M with reunion. Yeah. That's it. Hmmmm. I wonder if he's married.

In "offline" or "in-person" networking, it's crucial to show your face at events to build a rapport with other attendees. Online networking is similar: you want to be seen "around town." In this case, town could mean the entire World Wide Web, which, of course, is enormous. But, when you really break it down into the important places for online networkers to be, the web can be easily and efficiently navigated.

There are a few websites that can build your online reputation quickly and effectively, so all you need to do is focus on those. Just like every teenager seems to be either on Facebook or MySpace, we believe every professional should post a profile on at least one major professional networking site. Our favorites are LinkedIn.com (for general business networking) and a relevant niche site, like the Publishers Marketplace member directory for writers, Women for Hire's Career Network for job hunters, and Downtown Women's Club's DWC Plus member directory for women in business. Of course you can use the tips in this chapter for other professional networking sites, such as Ryze.com, or a social network at a membership association to which you belong.

Not sure which one to choose? Start by researching where your colleagues and potential contacts "hang out." Either search for their names online or simply ask a colleague. You can also do some searching by industry on most online networks without signing up. For example, if you're looking for decision makers in the health care industry, go to a networking site's "search" page and put in a job title, e.g., "CFO" and "health care." Or better yet, you can take a moment before deleting the next email invitation you receive to join a network and check it out. Different industries will have different networks where they are prevalent. This is probably because a few active and really connected networkers in a particular industry selected the one they liked and then brought along all their contacts.

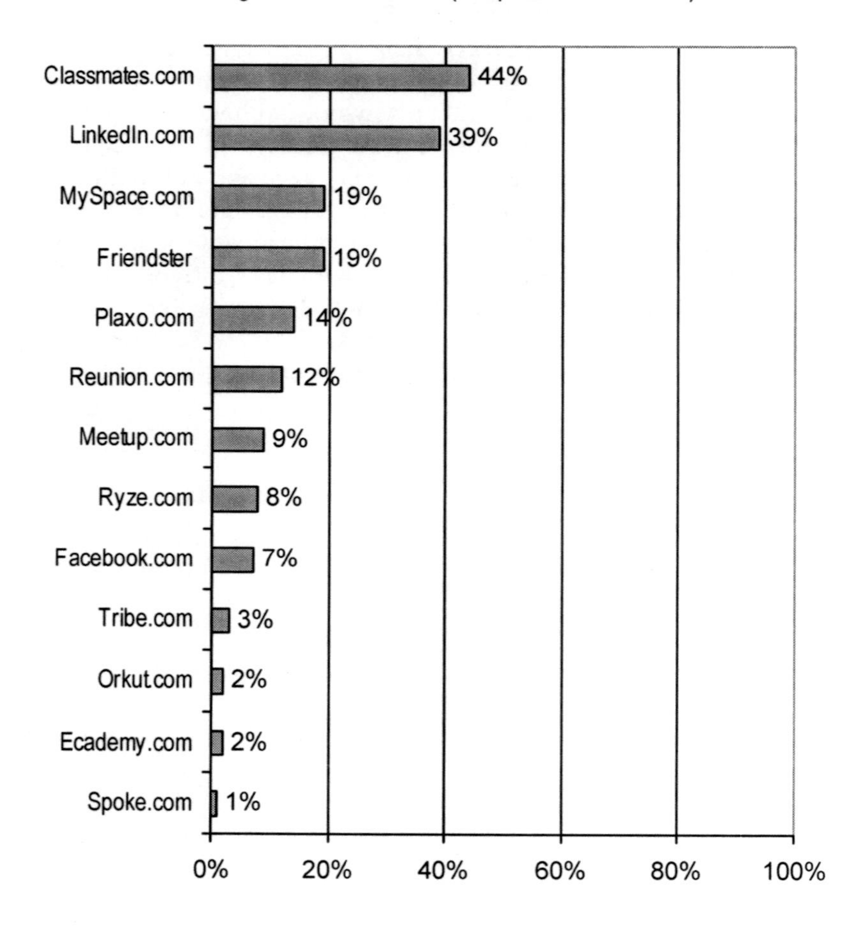

Excerpted from the DowntownWomensClub.com 2006 Online Networking Survey.

Think Links

LinkedIn.com, one of the leaders in professional networking, helps you connect with former colleagues, alumni, and friends, as well as make new connections to recommended job candidates, industry experts, and business partners. It might help to think of LinkedIn and similar sites as a big online cocktail party where everyone is walking around with their resume plastered on their backs. You get to review some basic profile information and members can easily customize their public profile view. However, you only get the full story if you and that person share a mutual acquaintance willing to introduce the two of you.[20]

But wait, there's more. Let's say you're still wandering around that cocktail party checking out everyone's basic information when you see someone whose resume has a flashing green light on it that matches a flashing green light you have. This means that you have something in common. It could be that you once worked at the same company, attended the same school, or perhaps you currently belong to the same business association. All of which makes going up and saying "hi" a lot easier than picking someone at random.

Or, maybe you see someone walking around with a great big flashing blue light. No, you're not in Kmart and it's not a discount on diapers; instead, what if that blue light means that person is hiring on behalf of their company? Wouldn't that be great to know? Especially if you're job hunting—that's the kind of blue-light special you'd be interested in hearing more about. On LinkedIn, recruiters and employers who are hiring are easily identifiable.

Now, we're not fans of literally walking around in public with our resumes plastered on us (although, it might have crossed at least one of our minds during an unemployed stint in the late eighties and early nineties). And, neither of us would wear flashing lights, even during the holidays. But, that's the beauty of online social networks. We can change what information we want public about ourselves and also

---

[20] Note that there are ways to introduce yourself to individuals you don't know. However, online networks like LinkedIn have many restrictions and guidelines for doing so.

check things out at our convenience (often late at night with Jon Stewart on the TV for company) and with a huge amount of privacy. Then we can take our time "linking up" to people with whom we want to have ongoing business relationships, or reconnecting with people from our pasts.

Getting Down to Business on a Social Network

To get started on an online social network, you must register (most are free; although some social networks offer upgraded premium accounts). Then, you take a few minutes to create your own personal profile that is essentially a beefed-up version of your resume or CV that other people will see when they find you through a search of your name or keywords contained in your profile. Different sites allow you to include different elements in your profile, but you will generally have room to include:

- Professional credentials (your resume)
- Industry categorization
- Professional areas of expertise
- Types of people with whom you are interested in connecting
- Types of opportunities that interest you
- Organizations to which you belong
- Awards and honors you've received
- Interests and hobbies
- Endorsements (short comments, written by one connection for another, about work the two of you shared in a particular position; or a list of other members with whom you've done business)

Note that unlike social networking sites, LinkedIn profiles do not include photographs, but some other professional networking sites do.

Once your profile is posted on a site, you can start connecting with people you know and asking them to be a part of your network. Remember the Six Degrees of Separation from Kevin Bacon game we talked about in the last chapter? Well, this is Six Degrees of Separation from You. The focus is on taking your existing network and expanding your connections through links to networks of the people already in your own network. This way, you aren't being contacted by total strangers; instead, you make new contacts with the help of a trusted connection while protecting your privacy, your inbox, and your existing professional relationships.

You can use LinkedIn, and other similar social networks, to connect in several ways—all for free at the basic registration level. Below is a list of ways we've discovered to use LinkedIn to build our networks as well as to find information about our industries.

- **Invite people to join your network who are already on LinkedIn.** Chances are you already have a large network of friends and colleagues who are members of LinkedIn. In that case, after you join, you can search for them and send invitations to connect with you. Once they're in your network, then you can view and connect with their contacts. However, you can't contact anyone unless you go through your friends to make the introduction. This also means that no one can contact your network without going through you.

- **Upload your email contact database.**[21] Uploading your email contact database will tell you which of your contacts is already on LinkedIn and makes it easy for you to send out a limited number of invitations to connect. (The invitation limitation is one of the many safeguards professional networking websites have against spammers.) If certain people aren't on LinkedIn, you can send them invitations to join LinkedIn and after they join, they can accept your invitation to be part of your network.

- **Search for people you would like to meet through keywords.** When you type in a keyword or phrase, such as "graphic designer" or "Phi Beta Kappa," LinkedIn will generate a list of people on the

[21] Outlook, Yahoo, Gmail, AOL, and most other major contact databases can be uploaded.

website whose profiles contain that word or phrase. LinkedIn will also tell you how many "degrees" those people are away from you and through which of your contacts. You can then reach out to the specified contact and ask that person to forward along your desire for an introduction.

- **Find former colleagues and classmates**. If you input the content from your resume (the basis of the LinkedIn profile), LinkedIn will tell you which of your former colleagues and classmates (college and graduate school) are also on LinkedIn based on the years you were in school or employed at that company. You can then contact your former colleagues via the site. You will not see that person's email address until he or she has accepted your invitation (unless that person has chosen the option to list it as part of his or her public profile). Connecting with former colleagues is one of the most common ways that people connect through LinkedIn. It's like Classmates.com, but for former workmates.

- **Research companies**. Pamela Campagna, president of BLUE SAGE Consulting, Inc. says that she uses LinkedIn to research people, positions, and companies. "I often turn to LinkedIn to identify people in my network who might work at a potential consulting customer," she explains. "Aside from the obvious opportunity to 'network into' an organization through people in your network, it's often just as useful to understand how many people no longer work at an organization. If a particular prospect is on LinkedIn, you can also get an idea of their background and inclinations by studying their profile. Based on their background, what are their likely biases? Are they weak in operations or strong in sales? What might be their span of control in their company? Advanced research helps in preparing for that first client meeting."

- **Use LinkedIn as an online focus group.** Another research idea from Pamela is to reach out to people in your LinkedIn network for help: "The 'question and answer' feature [which can be accessed through the LinkedIn Answers tab] is a great addition. I've recently posted a technical question to my network to get ideas for an upcoming conference. Not only have I received knowledgeable responses, but I can also follow up with those in my extended network who have responded." We also tested this out and found it to be one of the best features of the website!

- **Connect with your favorite affinity group via the site.** If you're a member of an affinity group like DowntownWomensClub.com's DWC LinkedIn Group, you can send an invitation to other group members directly, even if there is no link between you. By signing up as part of such a group, you are also inviting other people in the same group to reach out to you. However, note that you will not see other group members' email addresses until they have accepted your invitation (unless that person has chosen the option to list it as part of his or her public profile).

These are only a few of the many ways to use LinkedIn, and most of the tips apply to any professional networking website you might choose to join.

Savvy Tip #23: Think of LinkedIn and other social networks as an address book that updates itself. With today's transient population, sometimes email addresses are the most consistent contact method. With social networks, the onus is on the members to keep their own information up-to-date.

Since LinkedIn is all about networking, we decided to reach out and network with the folks at that company. Orly Keren, marketing manager for LinkedIn, was kind enough to chat with us and provide some insider tips on how to make the most of this professional networking web community.

Q: How do you describe LinkedIn to people who are unfamiliar with your services?
A: LinkedIn is the best way to keep in touch with people who you already know and trust, and it enables you to build your professional network for future opportunities. Professionals use LinkedIn to get business done everyday. Whether you're looking for answers to your questions, service providers, venture capital, new clients for your business, talented candidates for a position on your team, or other career development opportunities, LinkedIn is the world's largest professional community. By joining the network, you can reconnect with past colleagues, alumni, and peers and be a part of the growing global community.

Q: What would you tell people who have security concerns about networking online?
A: We place the highest amount of attention to security. You control the content in your own profile, and you have the option of selecting what information you want available in your public profile.

Q: What are the most effective ways that people use LinkedIn to build their networks?
A: For some, the art of social networking is built into their DNA. Connecting with people and fostering relationships happens intuitively. LinkedIn allows "connectors" to do what they do best, only more efficiently, effectively, and online. For those who shy away from cocktail party encounters, LinkedIn provides these professionals with the smartest, most intimate way to be "in." For others, LinkedIn is a way to anchor serendipitous encounters. The power of being in touch with people is just a click away.

Q: What are the most effective ways that people use LinkedIn to keep in touch with/maintain their existing networks?
A: In addition to connecting with others, many people use LinkedIn to build their own personal brand, leverage connections, raise their online profile, and even to help meetings run smoother.

Build "brand you." You own your profile. So take a moment to add as much relevant information to your profile as possible. Showcase your experience, achievements, and contributions. Also promote your work by adding a link to your blog or website. It's a great way for you to market yourself to the world and build "brand you."

Leverage connections. Did you know that people with more than 20 connections are 34 times more likely to be approached with a job opportunity than people with less than five? Be sure to connect with people you know and trust, such as alumni, current and former colleagues, and clients. Growing your network can help increase the chances that people will see your profile first when they're searching for someone to hire or do business with. Likewise, growing your connections enables you to gain greater visibility into the network. This will help with your own proactive career development or your own search for prospective clients. Being connected is more than just the best way to stay in touch. It allows you to be accessible and ready for opportunities.

Get noticed. It's a competitive market out there, so enhance your profile by adding recommendations and keywords that will help you rank higher in search results. Endorsements, for example, will help you stand out from the crowd. People are naturally more inclined to hire or do business with professionals who are recommended. Also, sprinkle your profile with keywords relevant to your industry. It's important to highlight your skills, and being savvy about search engine optimization will work to your advantage.

Make meetings go smoother. Use LinkedIn to do pre-meeting homework. Prior to meeting with a hiring manager, candidate, or potential client, look up their LinkedIn profile to learn about their business, talents, and personal interests. Knowing more personalized details about the individual you're meeting with can help eliminate awkward moments of silence and help facilitate the conversation.

Q: Can you explain the "Answers" feature on LinkedIn?
A: The "Answers" feature allows you to tap into a brain trust of over 11 million members. Any LinkedIn member can post an industry-specific question. Then other members reply. By answering questions yourself, you build your own expertise. Answers can be posted publicly or sent through a private message. It's not only an efficient way to get answers to your questions, but also a reliable means to quickly access quality information as well.

Q: Can you network internationally on LinkedIn?
A: Yes, we are a global network. There is one LinkedIn for all countries, which is phenomenal. It's a global village. You can use Answers, for example, to ask questions about relocating to a new country. Whether it's Australia, Japan, or Italy, you're pretty much guaranteed to get a response from someone in your destination country. We have many success stories of members seeking advice through Answers and then fostering relationships through that initial contact. Getting a credentialed introduction to someone through your network is another way to conduct business, both locally and internationally.

Q: Do you have any specific tips for job seekers using LinkedIn?
A: LinkedIn puts a job seeker's personal network to work. It allows you to leverage your contacts and those of the people you know. Make sure to keep your information on your profile current. Sprinkle your profile with keywords, be sure to get recommendations [also known as endorsements], and add as many relevant details as possible; all of these factors will help you rank higher in search results. You can also tap into Answers for advice on your job search or business.

For people looking to hire someone, LinkedIn has a talented pool of active and passive candidates. Review candidates' profiles regarding how they wish to be contacted and what opportunities they are interested in (the information is located at the bottom of every user's profile).

Those looking for jobs or to hire people can also get competitive information; you can gauge the health of the industry and other companies through LinkedIn. Be sure to use the Advanced Search tab to search for helpful information.

We realize that it's hard to read about technical applications in a book, so we hope you go online and test some of these ideas out for yourself. In order to further encourage that, we've also asked Nancy Loderick, who monitors the Downtown Women's Club's LinkedIn Group, to share a helpful FAQ section she created for the membership related to networking on LinkedIn:

Q: Should I try to get as many connections as I can?
A: A few qualified (or known) connections can be far more useful, and manageable, than hundreds of "unknowns."[22] If you need to specifically talk to a person, you want to reconnect with someone, or you think you will be contacting that person frequently in the future, then it's appropriate to invite him or her to be in your network.

Q: What's the best way to invite someone into your network?
A. Please note that people tend to ignore "mass" invitations that are generic and not specifically directed at an individual. Be sure to customize the basic "Would you like to join my network" email that LinkedIn offers. People are more likely to respond to a personal request.

Q: What is the most effective way to use LinkedIn?
A: You will get better results if in your invitation to connect, you are specific as to why you want to connect with this person, e.g., looking for a web designer or moving to London, etc. It is also a

[22] On LinkedIn, you might see people stating that they are "open networkers." This means that they believe in linking to as many people as possible to increase their networks. Personally, we don't agree with this approach, but clearly it works well for others.

good idea to offer your new contacts something in return, whether it is offering to refer other clients or something else that would help them out.

Q: What if someone invites me to link up and I don't know the person?
A: We recommend only linking to people you have a reason to link to and vice versa. If someone invites you to be in his or her network and gives no specific reason, you should feel free to ignore or decline.

Savvy Tip #24: Think carefully about whom you invite into your network, because you will be exposing your other contacts to that person. When in doubt, use the "dinner with friends" test. If you don't know certain people well enough to invite them out to a dinner with your friends and close colleagues, then you might not want to invite them into your online network either.

Wendy's World, Monday, 9:30 a.m. *Well, well, well. What do you know? Mr. Homecoming King two years running has accepted my LinkedIn invitation. Time to check out his network. Still wish they had pictures on LinkedIn. So, who does Chris Martin know? Tommy Harrons? Jake Sullivan? Huh. Weren't they from high school? Is anyone in his network NOT from high school? Funny, I only keep in touch with M. But, she'll be thrilled to contact this group. Guess I'll email Chris the reunion details and ask him to spread the word. Wonder if he's married.*

Put Your Best Face Forward

Despite having a LinkedIn group, DowntownWomensClub.com developed their own member directory called DWC Plus. Why? First, because they cater to a niche market, female professionals, but also because as mentioned earlier, they surveyed their members and found that the top two reasons that these women did NOT network online were because (1) it was too impersonal; and (2) they couldn't leverage their image and personality.

The DWC Plus member directory and other similar services like Ziggs.com try to make the professional profile a little more personal. On both, you're able to post a photo and include information that tells a little bit more about your personality, like your favorite motto, professional mission or signature line, and favorite websites.

On your DWC Plus profile, you can list other DWC Plus members you've done business with, which is similar to the endorsements given on LinkedIn. In addition, DWC Plus and Ziggs automatically submit your profiles to Google and other search engines.[23] This allows people who may have tossed or lost your business card to go online through any search engine and find information about you that you yourself have posted. Now, we still know people who don't want to be found on the web. And while some might have a valid reason (witness protection programs do have strict requirements), when it comes to business, remember that the Internet is the new Yellow Pages, and that's where colleagues, clients, and employers are going to look for you.

One of the most important elements when posting your profile is to think about keywords. Keywords are the terms that people might put in when searching for you, or for someone like you who provides services that they need. For example, if you practice law, you might want to include both "attorney" and "lawyer" as well as the type of law you practice. Do you also give talks and workshops? Then you might want to include "speaker" or "professional trainer."

Savvy Tip #25: Know the key to keywords. Most people looking online for service providers search by keywords, whether in a

[23] LinkedIn and other social networks have also started adding a "publicly viewable" option, which will allow search engines to find and list their profiles.

search engine like Google or within a social network. Make sure you come up with as many keywords as someone might use to find you and then include these somewhere in your profile description. Check out keywords of someone in your industry for ideas; there are no copyright laws on keywords (yet!). Or, ask a friend what keywords they might use if they were looking for someone with your skill set and services.

Here are a few additional suggestions for maximizing the value of your profile:

- **Promote it.** Include a link to your professional profile as part of your signature line in emails so people can click on your profile, learn more about you, and increase your Googleability to boot!

- **Include links.** Within your profile, you can include the URLs of articles you've written, organizations you're part of, and events where you're speaking.

- **Get personal.** All work and no play makes for a boring profile. You can market your business, but you can also market other pursuits, such as nonprofit work, creative writing, sports, pottery, or pretty much anything else. Just remember to keep your content and images professional.

Be a Joiner

Does all of this sound a little overwhelming? That's often the case with busy professionals. So, here's our advice if all of this seems like too much extra work: Pick one, just one, social network to join. Use the steps outlined in the beginning of this chapter to find where your most desirable contacts are posting their profiles and join that one.

After you join, most social networks have some free basic services, but they may charge minimal amounts (compared to more expensive in-person networks) to get services like the ability to contact people or to have your profile submitted to search engines. Once you belong, immediately post at least your contact information. Hopefully you'll give yourself enough time to put a little more than that, but it's O.K. to take small steps. Just go back for a few minutes every day and update and expand your profile information.

That's one of the great things about online profiles on social networks: You can continue to tweak and craft your online resume as often as you want. We also recommend having a friend check it out every once in a while to see what she thinks (or catch any typos!). Then, each week, set aside 30 minutes to explore the network and its different services. For example, the first week, look for people from your alma mater. The next week, try searching for employees of a former employer. Then after that, either send out one contact email a day, or go for five in an afternoon.

If after a few months you're not getting much benefit from the network you've joined, try a different one. There are endless networks out there and more are launching every day. Once you find your way online, you'll never "tap out" your network ever again.

Chapter 6: Click and Get Hired

Wendy's World, Wednesday, 4:40 pm. *I hate my job, I hate my job, I hate my job. I'm being sent to Delaware for my next assignment. Delaware! Companies incorporate there, no one actually has a headquarters there. Do they? Well, except one of our clients, of course. That's it. I'm posting my profile on that job board on that women's business website. It protects your privacy, and I hear the recruiters like boards with currently employed job hunters. Besides, I definitely can't afford to lose this job before landing the next. Perhaps while I'm stuck in Delaware at another generic Residence Away From Home with lots of downtime, I'll get online and start researching more job sites.*

Since many online networkers are seeking job opportunities, we wanted to dedicate some space to that specific type of networking. Professional networking sites are becoming particularly popular places for job hunters to make connections and for recruiters to find candidates. If you're a job hunter or a recruiter, registering for these boards is essential. But are professional networking sites better than traditional job sites, such as Monster.com or CareerBuilder.com? Nancy Loderick, DWC's director of network partnerships, shares her experience and advice from a job search she conducted:

"Having used both LinkedIn and job boards. I found all of these tools work best when used in conjunction with each other. I've looked at job boards, such as Monster, 6figurejobs, etc., to see which companies are hiring. I didn't necessarily see exact positions for what I would be looking for, but general trends. For example, I might do a search for "client relationship" positions and see what companies list positions. More often than not, these positions are the more junior positions. But, this has given me a sense of which companies are hiring.

> Once I developed a list of companies that are hiring, I would try to find a contact at these companies by using my LinkedIn network, as well as my other networks, to find contacts (other networks would include my alumni association, DWC, and friends) who work at those companies. The contacts may not necessarily work in the department that I would be interested in, but they can be a great source of information about the company in general. And, they may know the hiring manager of the department I want."

Nancy's advice is echoed on the other side of the equation: company hiring managers. Maureen Crawford Hentz, manager of talent acquisition for OSRAM SYLVANIA, a lighting products company, shares some insider tips for online job hunters:

> "I would say at this point that 80% of our recruiting comes from online sources. ... OSRAM SYLVANIA uses large commercial sites, niche sites, and online networking tools to find candidates. Our recruiters are also skilled in deep-web searching—finding leads on passive candidates [who do not post their resumes on employment websites].
>
> It's important to understand that recruiters will now use all technologies available to find candidates. Many recruiters I know routinely Google candidates for background information. ZoomInfo, DowntownWomensClub.com, and LinkedIn are common sites visited.
>
> My best advice for candidates is to get your information out there, but carefully. When working on one of the big job boards, make sure you understand keyword loading, as recruiters use those boards by searching for keywords. This is the same strategy you want to employ when applying for jobs via company websites: use a number of keywords so that your resume can be found. Recruiters search their own resume databases by keywords as well."

Savvy Tip #26: (From Expert, Maureen Crawford Hentz) Privacy is key. I recommend to clients that they never put down a home address or phone number on a resume posted in a public place (one of the big job boards for example), but rather set up an email account just to receive job inquiries. Then be sure to check that account often. My general rule of thumb: If you wouldn't post the information on a bulletin board at the supermarket, don't post it online.

In-house recruiting executives are not the only ones trolling the web for employees. If you're hoping to attract the attention of a headhunter through your online networking efforts, you'll be interested in these comments from Scott White, vice president of Chaloner Associates, an executive search firm with a national focus on communications, marketing, and investor relations:

> "My colleagues and I use a variety of technologies to identify candidates and then communicate with them. …We are constantly looking for ways to use the web more creatively and effectively. We are active in industry networking groups—their online member directories are helpful, but we also find that staying current on news and trends can help us identify thought leaders and those who are the best networked within their field or industry.
>
> When we write an effective email to reach out for referrals or candidates, we get a very good response—much better than the old direct mail standard response rate. We also track when someone joins an organization or when someone is promoted—it's a nice excuse to make an introduction or re-connect with someone with whom we worked in the past.
>
> We find that scouring press releases is helpful, too. We set up Google alerts that flag specific companies, industries, or keywords to make sure we don't miss any announcements. Again, these releases provide contact information as well as information about

developments in an industry. ZoomInfo.com is a great site, either to identify potential candidates/referral sources or to get current contact information for someone we can't track down. LinkedIn.com is another great tool for us.

We also scan workshop brochures to see who the speakers and industry thought leaders are, and we reach out to them. We find articles, press releases, MySpace pages, alumni information, and more. Results from searching through job boards and other online sources are infinitely variable. Two people might try the same search in a resume bank and get very different results."

While Scott's company makes great use of technology, he is also an advocate of the "clicks & mix" philosophy (combining online with in-person networking). He reminds us that, "Technology is a great way to identify people and perhaps to make initial contact, but there's no substitute for a face-to-face meeting and we do this as much as possible."

Both Maureen and Scott's comments confirm the importance of appearing in a variety of places online and of occasionally searching for yourself—using the same search engines that recruiters and HR executives use to find you. If you can't find yourself in these goldmines, then job opportunities can't find you either.

Savvy Tip #27: Online networking is a crucial component of any job hunt. Recruiters, hiring managers, small business owners, and anyone else looking for strong job candidates are bound to look online, so make sure your name comes up in their searches. Use job boards to find the keywords related to your desired job, and then include those words or phrases in your online resume, your professional network profiles, and anywhere else you appear online.

What's the next phase for online recruiting? Susan P. Joyce, the editor of Job-Hunt.org, an early pioneer in online job hunts, sees that the ease of responding to job postings online is pushing recruiters to niche sites. "If [a recruiter] posts a job on one of the large sites," she says "[they're] inundated within an hour—and mostly by unqualified candidates."

How do you stay on top of a variety of sites? Susan suggests checking a "job aggregator" site like Indeed.com, where you can run searches for specific terms like "brand managers" in New York City. "You'll instantly see who's posted jobs on company sites plus Monster, CareerBuilder, Dice, association sites, newspaper sites, etc. all in one search," says Susan. She also gives us this great insider's tip: "If an employer is posting jobs on Monster AND CareerBuilder AND the company website, then filling that job is a high priority."

Susan recommends keeping track of targeted employers or key executives at those companies by using the Google Alerts we discussed in Chapter Three. Register the company or individual's name, and then every time they're mentioned on the web, you'll receive a notice by email. Not only will you be up-to-date on happenings at your targeted company, you may even discover information that you can use as an excuse to reach out to a contact you might have there.

Companies are also starting to look for qualified candidates by posting job listings on blogs that are relevant to a certain industry, and through sites like H3.com, where recruiters can enlist "referral networks" of individuals who will then forward job postings to their contacts in exchange for cash rewards if they find an appropriate job candidate.

As you can see, the Internet offers incredible opportunities to find new networking contacts and to maintain and strengthen your current network. And, truthfully, the technology and strategies behind many of these sites are still evolving, so who knows what the future holds.

Chapter 7: Blog Blog Blog

Wendy's World, Friday, 10:05 p.m. *Yes, it's Friday and there is absolutely nothing on the telly. Admittedly this is normally my TiVo night (sad, I know!), but something happened and all of this week's programs are gone, non-existent, disappeared, vaporized... Sniff. O.K., it's no sense crying over a broken TiVo. Hmmmm. Guess I could catch up on emails. Besides, I owe BD guy another top five list. His latest email asked me which five blogs I read. Now, that's a bit personal isn't it? Although I suppose it's not that much different from his last question about my top five favorite books. I nearly fell off my couch when he responded to my Jane Austen fanaticism with a preference for more contemporary writers like Carl Hiaasen. Hell, I don't care what his preference in books is; I was absolutely stunned that he has actually read five books (and no mention of* The DaVinci Code*).*

Perhaps I will check out his blogs of choice. (Boy, has life changed when you check out a man's blogs, but not his butt). Although, maybe I need to diversify my own blog list before I send it; not sure he'll appreciate the humor of a gay guy from Detroit dishing on celebs in "Pink Is The New Blog"; or the fashion finds in BlogdorfGoodman. But, what can I say? A gal has to stay informed on celebrities and shopping! Hmmmmm. Perhaps I should throw in the dailyKOS, just so he knows where I stand on political issues and doesn't think I'm a shallow nitwit. Although, come to think of it, why do I even care what BD guy thinks?

Whenever you stumble across people saying "blog this, blog that," do you react like the Peanuts characters who hear only "Wanh, wanh, wanh, wanh, wanh" when adults talk? Well, take heart, because you're not alone. But it's time for you to take your fingers out of your ears and really listen to all the blog babble, because blogs are here to stay. Moreover, if you don't, when all those Gen Y employees finally outnumber you in the office, then all they'll be hearing when you talk is "Wanh, wanh, wanh, wanh, wanh."

Many of us are uncomfortable with this whole new world of social networking and blogging. Yet, that's par for the course when a new innovation comes along that changes how we do things. Think: answering machines, the Sony Walkman, and cell phones. Weren't these uncomfortable at first? But now even many of our grandparents have adopted at least two out of the three, and some may have even skipped over the Walkman and gone straight to the iPod. So, before Granny starts describing all the embarrassing things you did in your youth on her "Grannyblog," it's time to take a deep breath, walk to the end of the diving board and at least stick your toe in the water.

What is a blog? To be very basic, a blog is an online journal where someone puts down his or her opinions, thoughts, or random musings on a regular basis for others to read. Why is it called a blog? Because that's slang for "web log."

Remember William Shatner before he became *Boston Legal's* Denny Crane? Think back to when he commanded the galaxy as Captain Kirk and kept his Captain's Log, Star Date 2165. This was probably kept on a computer somewhere and if it was published to the crew, it would count as a blog. Of course, we'd much rather read a blog by Shatner's Denny Crane character, Mad Cow disease and all, rather than Captain Kirk, but we can't speak for the millions of Trekkies still out there.[24]

---

[24]Surfing a few blogs, we even found a post on Google's Official Blog to support our theory that Captain Kirk was a blogger: "Did you ever realize that among many other things, *Star Trek* predicted blogs? Think about it—all those 'Captain's log' and 'personal log' entries that Kirk would make. He was definitely a blogger. And of course the communicator-inspired cell phone design. And the crew was constantly asking the ship's computer for information...sort of like Google." Posted by Tom Galloway, Technical Writer, http://googleblog.blogspot.com/2006/08/stardate-081706.html.

In the following section we briefly look at different types of blogs, and why people may have them. However, our focus is on how everyone – even non-bloggers – can network through blogs.

While we're undertaking to write about blogging, please note that our focus is not going to be on how to run your blog, but solely on how to network with blogs, even if you don't run one yourself.[25]

Blogs as News Sources

These are the blogs that are keeping the Fourth Estate (newspapers and news producers) up at night. And it's not just that reporters are reading them to find out what stories to cover the next day, it's that they're worried that this is where people are getting their news now. Blogging allows for "user generated content," or UGC, on the web. That means people like us can post "news" online.

The issue with allowing the vox populi to post "news" is clearly whether the news can be trusted. Unlike a television network, which can be taken to task for misreporting a story, there is no reason a blogger can't post a conspiracy theory about 9/11 without any factual data. There is really no reprimand for a blogger posting speculative or even false news. Such is the reason that blogging as news can be a scary proposition for many. Samples of popular blogs where people get news include:

- BoingBoing: a weblog of "cultural curiosities and interesting technologies"
- The Huffington Post: the news as written by Arianna Huffington and other writers
- Daily Kos: State of the Nation: a daily weblog with political analysis on U.S. current events from a liberal perspective
- Instapundit: opinions on current events, as well as humor and personal notes

[25] One "how-to" blogging book we like is: *The Corporate Blogging Book* by Debbie Weil (Penguin Portfolio, 2006).

Blogs as the New Company Website

Web denizens have always recognized that a website cannot be static. This was why they invented "flash" media, or ways to put animation and mini-movies on websites. Although, if you're anything like us, your finger is on the "skip" button within five seconds, even the first time you see the flash movie.[26] C'mon, we TiVo out our commercials on television, why would we allow ourselves to be forced to watch them online? Blogging, however, helped move websites from a passive, mostly static advertisement (much like a billboard or brochure), into something more of a JumboTron or news broadcast where the action is live and updated regularly.

In the old days (yes, that would be 2002), you would pay a graphic designer and IT team (or perhaps a neighborhood teenager) to write some "code" and translate a design on paper onto a website. Any updates would take not just a huge part of your marketing budget, but often days, weeks, and sometimes months to implement. Unless you had a full-time staff member dedicated to the website, clients or visitors to the site would come back month after month only to view the same exact information.

Now, for mere pennies per day, you yourself can implement a blog and update your website immediately and on a regular basis. In fact, depending on what type of business you are running, you might be able to skip the whole website bit and just run a blog. Today, many of the blogging sites have ready-made templates and hosting capabilities, and if you can use an online program to design and send an e-newsletter, you can design a blog site in a few hours with easy-to-use programs such as WordPress.com, TypePad.com or Blogger.com.

Blogs as Marketing Tools

Earlier, we wrote about e-newsletters and how they can be used to interact with clients and networking contacts. Well, what about all

---

[26] Another potential downside to using flash technology to liven up your website is that search engines cannot pick up flash content.

those people out there whose spam blockers stop e-newsletters from getting through? Dynamic content, relevant to your business, can cause not only search engines, but actual people to find your site. It's a way to present yourself as an expert and provide valuable information for others. Even if you're just linking to relevant articles on others' sites.

For example, the Downtown Women's Club re-launched their original blog, formally known as the DWC Scoop, as the Women's DISH at www.womensdish.com, which tracks issues relevant to all women in the workplace as well as announcements geared to club members. The goal for the blog is not only to keep members informed, but also to draw new members who find out about the club through the blog.

Linda Merrill, owner of Chameleon Interiors, an interior design firm, runs a blog called ::Surroundings::, which focuses on design. She began including reviews of the BravoTV design show, *Top Design*, and attracted a following that even included one of the show's judges, Margaret Russell, editor-in-chief of *Elle Décor*. Russell subsequently mentioned Linda's blog in her magazine. Now, that's one way to raise your online image!

According to Kirsten Osolind, CEO of RE:INVENTION Marketing, a marketing and PR firm, your blog should benefit your business by focusing on the following four "Cs":

- Credibility building. If you regularly publish insights into your industry, you start to become known as an "expert."
- Cutting through marketing noise and clutter. Not everyone has a blog, so it's still a differentiator.
- Customer conversations. Blogs can spark and engage ongoing dialogues with clients and potential customers.
- Community building. You can use your blog to build a community, with both clients as well as other bloggers in the blogosphere.

Blogs as Personal Expression

At first we wanted to title this subsection, "Blogging as Art." But, we quickly rejected that idea as 99% of what's out there in the blogosphere could hardly be considered art. Yet, people blog for the same reasons they paint, write poetry, or take photos. It's a form of self-expression.

Some blogs are infamous: Washingtonienne spilled the guts about sex inside the beltway, PerezHilton.com "outs" gay celebrities, and Gawker.com snarks (gossips in a nasty way) about everyone on earth. Yet others actually offer serious opinions and chronicle important events. We, in fact, found several blogs devoted to our dear Jane Austen: www.austenblog.com, austentatious.blogspot.com, and janeaustenquotes.typepad.com.

This is all very exciting, but let's stop for a quick reality check. The fact is, out of the 12 million estimated blogs out there[27], except for the few popular blogs, the average blog is only read by a handful of readers.[28] Of course that doesn't—and shouldn't—stop people from putting content on the web.

What makes a good blog? It's all in the "blog fodder." That's a term for the type of informal writing and topics that appear in blogs. Believe it or not, there are blogs about plastic surgery, being a groom, crying while eating, comments people write on money (literally), and pretty much anything you can think of (or, in the latter two examples, topics that wouldn't even have crossed your mind).

Who is writing all this blog fodder? Of the millions, 99% are not as famous or well-spoken as Seth Godin (sethgodin.typepad.com) or Andrew Sullivan (andrewsullivan.theatlantic.com) or Arianna Huffington (www.huffingtonpost.com), but everyone can still benefit from the practice.

---

[27] This number is from a July 2006 PEW Internet & American Life Project report called *Bloggers: A Portrait of the Internet's New Storytellers*, and only accounts for American bloggers.

[28] According to the PEW Internet Bloggers study (mentioned in the preceding footnote), only 13% of bloggers surveyed reported having more than 100 hits per day.

If you're a blogger or aspiring blogger, here are some of our favorite tips for making sure your blog is the best it can be:

1. **Be topical, yet true to your focus.** If you can tie your blog comments to headline news in some way, it's more likely people will find you. However, keep your comments relevant, or you could lose your core customers/readers.
2. **Have an opinion.** Think about which blogs (or if you don't read blogs, which editorials) you read. Are they neutral or do they have an opinion? We bet it's the latter.
3. **Use keywords.** The Downtown Women's Club's WomensDISH receives a number of hits from people searching for blogs that include the term "the gender wage gap," "mommy wars," and other women's issues.
4. **Be consistent.** If you blog every other day, that's fine. But don't do a bunch of posts in one week and then let it slide for a couple of weeks. Bring in guest bloggers if you need the help to keep on track.
5. **Be conversational.** Blog writing differs from reporting or article writing. It's about creating a dialogue with your readers, who will hopefully respond with comments. Try reading your post out loud. If it sounds exactly like how you would say it, then post it!
6. **Don't bury the lead.** This is a key to all journalism, but in the world of the 10-second attention span, get to the most interesting point first or people will leave.
7. **Provide snappy headlines.** See the above tip. The funnier, wittier, and bolder the headline, the more likely it is to grab someone's attention. Also, headlines should be short because RSS feeds[29] often can fit only the first five or so words.

[29] RSS stands for Really Simple Syndication, which is when the headlines of a blog are published together on a website. If you have a MyYahoo, iGoogle, or other homepage, you can subscribe to your favorite blogs and see the most recent headlines updated in real time.

Blogs as Networking Tools

In our opinion, any technology becomes a networking tool when it can promote the interaction of people, and blogging is definitely a participatory technology. "Comments" boxes appear at the bottom of blog postings for a reason! Think of them as the Q&A section after a presentation by a speaker. Bloggers are practically begging you to ask a question, make a comment, or further the discussion.

Now, if you're like us, when you hear a fabulous speaker deliver a presentation, you're not the one who is grabbing the microphone to ask your question because that's just putting yourself so "out there." Nor are we likely to be the types to elbow our way through the crowds to engage the speaker on our own personal issues. Of course, even if we were so inclined, we don't have time because we have to dash off to that next meeting. But, if we have a minute or two later in the day, and that person has a blog, what could be an easier way to start a dialogue than writing a "comment"?

Savvy Tip #28: Meet the experts...online. If you hear a great speaker at an event, check to see if he or she has a blog. We've found that people who run their own blogs, no matter how popular and famous, are often very free with their answers and responses when someone comments on their blog.

Now let's dig in a little deeper into the etiquette of blog networking.

Blog Networking: Commenting on Others' Blogs

Think of commenting on blogs as writing letters to the editor. The only differences are that the likelihood of being published is nearly 100% (the blogger will usually have the option to approve or reject your comment, although rarely does a comment get rejected unless it's completely offensive); the chance of the blogger personally responding to your comment is fairly high; and the shelf life of your comment is much longer than a daily or weekly paper. All of these are networking advantages.

You can post comments on other people's blogs as part of introducing yourself. For instance, if there is a person you'd like to meet, you can read his or her blog, post a kind comment (everyone loves flattery), and then send an email citing your blog comment. Another great place to comment is on newspaper websites. Most columnists whose materials appear online include comment sections to engage readers. And, some, not all, even find the time to respond to comments, either right on the blog, via a direct email or in a future column.

You can also use comments to promote your expertise or even link to your own website or online profile. Be careful with this as it can appear pushy, but if people are commenting about a topic that's relevant to your expertise, by all means offer yourself as a resource. People who read blogs also read comments. This means you can attract the attention of not only the blogger, but also his or her readers.

Blog Networking: Running Your Own Blog

Running your own blog is an endeavor, although not as hard or time-consuming as you might expect. While there are books entirely devoted to this topic, here are some questions to ask yourself before you take on the responsibility:

- Do I want to learn something new on the computer?
- Do I have a business that would benefit from a more dynamic website?
- Do I want to represent myself as an expert in my field?
- Do I have a particular topic I could focus on that would be relevant to my business?
- Do I think I can churn out two to three sentences, three to four times per week on that topic?
- Do I understand that there is a fine line between self-promotion and informing the public of relevant information?

If you answered yes to all of those questions, then we recommend you test out the blogosphere. But remember, running a blog is like volunteering for an unpaid position. You can do yourself and your reputation a lot of good, but if you don't follow through, you can end up doing yourself in. What we'll do here is walk you through the process of getting started, so you can see that it's certainly "doable."

1. **Research the blogosphere.** Visit Technorati.com, Blogger.com, Google Blogs, or other blog search engines and type in the keywords you would use to describe your proposed blog. This will help you see what other blogs are out there following your topic. If you find a whole bunch of similar blogs to the topic you have in mind, don't let that discourage you. Yes, there are other marketing/finance/sales gurus in the world besides you. However, you can (and must) find a way to differentiate your blog. If the other blogger follows marketing issues in general, you could follow marketing issues relevant to a more targeted market, such as women, Baby Boomers, ethnic groups, financial marketing, etc. If it's finance, you could track certain issues or markets.

Savvy Tip #29: Befriend the competition. Stop thinking of these other blogs as competition, but instead, bookmark them as more resources to link to...and network with!

2. **Determine your modus operandi.** Decide whether you are going to be strictly news (i.e., simply providing a list of relevant stories to your market by writing "check this out..."), or if you are going to be a bit more opinionated, throwing in your personal opinion about the news or some relevant thoughts on a matter. The best blogs do reflect an individual's personality, so structure yours in a way that is comfortable to you.

3. **Name that blog!** Blogs tend to have clever names, or if your own name is well-known enough, it can just be known as "[Your

Name's] Blog." Keep in mind consistency with your brand as a person or a business owner. It's smart to name your blog after your company to build name recognition, or to include your name in the title. We suggest testing your blog name with a few people you would consider to be your target readers and see if the name is memorable and appealing. (Note that people will have to type your blog name on their keyboard, so you probably want to avoid something hard to spell, like, say, Onomatopoeia Daily.)

4. **Pick your platform.** You also need to decide which blogging platform (a.k.a., online service) to use. There are several out there with different price ranges and capabilities. The best way to decide which one to use is to find other people's blog designs you like and then check out what platform they're using (usually this is easily identifiable by a logo at the bottom of the blog). We've actually written to bloggers to ask why they've picked the service they did. As for the service level, we suggest starting with the most basic one and asking your friends for input before launching it to the world. If you have a tech team, you can have them incorporate your blog into your existing website, or, if you don't have a website, the blog can be your website. Most of the blogging software sites have easy-to-follow steps to put up a blog and start posting.

5. **Write that post.** For those of you unfamiliar with how to write blog posts, Wikipedia.com explains that a blog entry typically consists of the following:

- **Title:** the main title (headline) of the post.
- **Body:** the main content of the post.
- **Permalink:** the URL (link) of the full, individual article.
- **Post date:** the date and time the post was published.

A blog entry optionally includes the following:

- **Comments:** feedback from your readers, as discussed above.

- **Categories:** also known as "tags," categories reflect the subjects that the entry discusses. You can assign as many as you'd like for each blog post.
- **Trackback and/or Pingback:** links to other sites that refer to the entry (it is common blogging practice to link to any sites you mention or from which you cite content or ideas).

Just remember, if you start a blog, you have to maintain it. Period. Nothing is staler than a posting about Christmas lingering as your blog post in February. It's O.K. to write short postings, but be sure to keep your content fresh. And, don't forget to acknowledge and engage readers who either write comments or link to your blog (which you can find out through Technorati.com, a site where you can register and track your blog), or through a service like Google or Yahoo Alerts. If you can't write your blog at least once or twice each week, then blogging is probably not going to have much benefit for you as either a marketing or networking tool.

Savvy Tip #30: Make a schedule and stick to it. Most people will assume a blog will be updated daily, unless you have a news blog and that is updated frequently during the day. However, if you want to post weekly articles, that's fine too. Just make sure your readers expect that to be the schedule.

Blog Networking: Community Blogging

If running your own blog is not appealing or realistic for you, there are still other ways to get your words out on the web. You could work with some colleagues and do a "group" blog where everyone posts something weekly or can cover for each other when someone is out of the office. You can also publish your thoughts on a community blog such as CultureCloud.com or Gather.com, where pretty much anyone can submit short stories, images, or reports on any topic, which are then posted on your own personal page on the site.

When it comes to networking on community blogs, we turned to David Woodrow, vice president of groups at Gather.com. He gave us the following tips for building a social network on Gather.com (almost all of which can be applied to other similar community sites).

- **Get personal.** When you join Gather.com, it's important to complete your profile with as much information as you feel comfortable. You don't need to fill in all the questions, but at a minimum post your favorite books, music, and films. This enables people to get a better sense of you as a person. In this case, familiarity drives engagement. You also want to upload a small photo as an icon. This icon will appear next to your profile on your article pages and alongside any comments you make on the site.

- **Read and post**. As a member, you can participate in the community. Read articles that interest you and, when appropriate, share your thoughts by commenting. Most importantly, participate on Gather by posting articles. By writing on Gather, you are able to build your network and build broader exposure for your content. Your content will further enable you to leverage Gather's social networking functionality. Your posts can be any length, but generally run between 500–750 words. Remember to check back on your posts and respond to the comments from your readers. You don't need to respond to them all, but people really appreciate when you remain part of the conversation on Gather.

- **Create a network**. The power of social networking is through connections and networks. The larger your Gather network, the better enabled you are to benefit by people telling others about your work and sharing information—all automatically via Gather's messaging and connections system. Find people who share your interests and proactively ask them to connect to you. Or, send private messages to people you have met on Gather using Gather's messaging system.

- **Join and/or create groups**. Search for and join groups that deal with the topics you are interested in. Search for groups created by other people who are looking to network or start a networking group of your own and invite other people to join your group.

"To sum it up most simply," says David, "the single most powerful action for a person to gain popularity on Gather is to respond and engage with other members."

Blogging isn't for everyone, but if you're going to jump in and launch a blog yourself, dabble on a community blog, or even comment on other blogs, and remember to focus on the message you want to send to the world. Blogging is a dialogue with your audience and you want to be just as engaging, entertaining, and generous as you would be with any other type of networking.

Chapter 8: The Topic is Internet Forums…Discuss!

Wendy's World, Tuesday, 2:00 p.m. *Ugh. What a lunch. Chris Martin, my high school crush, excuse me, FORMER high school crush, who I found on LinkedIn, was in town on business and asked me to lunch. Then he turns out to be a total loser, whose only topic of conversation was some football game that took place 20 years ago. And, maybe my taste has changed, or some of us don't age quite as well, but the Chris Martin across the table from me was no "Chris Martin" that I remembered. Or perhaps it was the "tan line" on his ring finger that was so completely revolting. Ick. This is why when he suggested a drink at his hotel later, I bolted for the ladies room.*

To make matters worse, I then literally run into BD (Blind Date) guy as I trip on the way to the bathroom. Toss in the gorgeous blonde with the D&G suit and the Jimmy Choo shoes at his side and it was all I could do to slink off to the loo before my self-respect completely imploded. Which, of course, happened about three minutes later, when my iPod fell out of my purse and into the toilet. Ick. Ick. Ick.

Wendy's World, Tuesday, 2:25 p.m. *By the way, who was that tall glamazon at lunch with BD guy? Must be a client. Maybe a colleague? Perhaps it was a first date from an online dating site? Or...his wife? That cad! No, wait. Our first date was a set-up; my friends would know if he was married. Hmmmmm. Maybe I should drop him an email. I could make a witty joke about "running into him" and the iPod incident.*

Wendy's World, Tuesday, 2:35 pm. *What's this? BD guy with a prompt response. I like that. His sister thought I was cute? Even if I am a klutz? His sister?! And, he Googled "iPod fell in toilet."*

> *OMG.*[30] *This is too funny—an entire message board dedicated to what to do when you drop your iPod in the crapper. I'm not sure I want to try microwaving it, though. Perhaps I'll register as "ipodlvr" and ask if anyone had success sending a "crappy" iPod back to Apple.*

Internet forums, otherwise known as web forums, message boards, and/or bulletin boards, are another significant way people communicate online today. The concept is simple. Like an old-fashioned campus or community bulletin board, anyone can post messages for others to read or comment. Except that you can do this right from your computer without ever leaving your desk. Even better, your audience is much larger, more diverse, not geographically bound, and able to comment back immediately or over a period of time (no one will paper over your posting or rip it down).

People use Internet forums to ask questions (How do I stop the 12:00 from blinking on my DVD player?); make announcements (job listings, neighborhood happenings); post product and retailer reviews (eBay, Amazon purchases); get the scoop on companies where they might work (Does anyone actually use the flextime policy at that investment bank?) and even just to discuss current events (Did Jordin really deserve to win on *American Idol*?). Whether it's politics, reality shows, or a shared love of pug puppies, just like with blogs, there's somebody out there ready and willing to discuss it.

Internet forums can be good networking when you use them to gather information, find a resource, or research a client or company. They also provide marketing opportunities. Dani Nordin, owner of the graphic design and marketing firm called the zen kitchen in Somerville, Massachusetts, recommends that when you post on an Internet forum, you make sure your signature (the blurb at the end of your message) includes information about your business, including the web address

---

[30] OMG is an acronym for Oh My God.

and a blog URL[31] (if you have one). It's a great way to build recognition and Googleability.

In fact, one of Dani's most recent clients—as well as a request for an interview, which appeared in a popular marketing blog—came directly from a few posts she made at the HOW Design Forum (forum.howdesign.com) site. In addition, Dani says she's started getting new subscribers to her e-newsletter through contributions she has posted on that forum and from her articles on Gather.com, the community blog mentioned in the previous chapter.

You don't even have to participate to benefit from online forums; you can just read the content that other people have posted. Often you don't even have to register or provide any personal information to read postings. However, if you have something you want to post, you will likely need to register. This is not so that they can send you spam, but so that they can verify that you are a live person and are not, in fact, going to spam their message board. Most of the time, you just give a "username," which does not have to be your own name, and on some boards, you even get an "avatar" (an icon used to represent the user).

Internet forums are run by moderators. These are the people who created the board to serve their own special interest. Ninety-nine percent of the time this is something they do on the side and not their "day job." The 1% for whom this is their day job usually run an Internet forum for their company and their job is to moderate content. Some forums have multiple moderators, who help run specific areas of the board. But, most are self-regulated and rely on participants to help monitor messages and report anything completely off-topic (or off-color) to the moderator.

Please note that because of the loose regulation, you will sometimes run into what is referred to as an "Internet troll," or someone who just purposely goes in and disrupts Internet forums and other online activity. Clearly, these people have too much time on their hands, and are usually noted and kicked out of the forum. (Moderators can ban users who abuse the board.) If you come across such a troll, your best

---

[31] "URL" stands for "uniform resource locator." In other words, your online address that comes after the "http://".

bet is to ignore the offensive post and report it directly to the forum moderator. Like all trolls, they're just craving attention.

Tips for Posting on an Internet Forum/Message Board

For expertise about message boards, we asked Internet strategist and technology guru Lena West, CEO and founder of xynoMedia Technology, to give us a few pointers. She gave us the following:

- **Get to know the lay of the land.** Take some time to poke around the community. Check out all available resources until you have a firm grasp on the community's landscape.
- **Stop, read, and understand.** Pay attention to how others frame their posts (including subject lines) to the group. Is there a particular format that you need to follow?
- **Pick a decent (and professional) log-in ID name.** Many times communities use your log-in ID as your username (they don't always tell you this) and it would really stink to be stuck with prettyblondegrrl@yahoo.com as your username (a.k.a. "screen name") for a business community.
- **Lurk.** Silence is golden. Sit for a little while and watch the activity. Find out who the moderators are and learn the appropriate way to contact them. Review the membership profile area. Anyone there you'd like to meet? If so, make a short list and visit their websites so that you'll have something intelligent to say when you encounter them on the boards.
- **Get to know the key influencers.** You need to know who the centers of influence are and, to the extent that their work or personality resonates with you, get to know them.
- **Your signature (information that appears with your posts along with your username) shouldn't be longer than your posts.** Cute graphics, long-winded mission statements, and famous quotes are passé and the mark of a complete amateur. The same goes for smiley faces and other emoticons. Your name, email address, phone number, and website address are *plenty*. If people want the long story, they can visit your website.

- **Be a giver.** Don't just visit the community to ask for help. Assisting others to find solutions builds goodwill, especially when it's related to your area of expertise. Offer solutions and give of your off-the-clock time as often as you can. Build this kind of networking into your annual marketing plan and budget.
- **Know when to take it offline.** Don't bog down the rest of the community with personal exchanges. Ask if it's O.K. to contact someone offline to continue a particular conversation and provide your email address first to facilitate the connection.
- **Don't blatantly self-promote.** Many online communities have rules against this. Savvy businesspeople know how to tactfully work their pitch into advice or an answer.
- **Use the search function before posing your question.** There is usually a search button in the upper right hand corner of an Internet forum. Find out whether your question has already been answered.
- **Be clear.** Remember, the people reading your message do not have the benefit of knowing the back story of your post. Re-read your posts and ask yourself, "If I didn't know any additional information about this situation, would I be able to understand what's going on and offer assistance?"

Lena reminds us to always have our manners "on," just like any other time we're networking. And, as with any community, Lena advises that we "know when to move on. Keep your goals in sight and regularly re-evaluate if the community is meeting those needs."

Savvy Tip #31: Pick an appropriate online alias. If you'd like to remain anonymous, choose a username that is not easily identifiable to you. However, if the message board is directly related to your business and you would want people reading your comments to locate you, it's O.K. to use your full name. Here's a good rule of thumb: If you would feel comfortable putting your comment in the letters to the editor section of your local paper or business journal, then use your real identity. When in doubt, leave your real name out.

Four Types of Internet Forums and Message Boards

1. Discussion Boards

Discussion boards are forums that are of topical concern to people. They range from technology and pop culture, to business, politics, makeup, fashion, and beyond. If a particular thought has ever crossed your mind, we guarantee someone, somewhere is online discussing it.

Discussion boards are distant cousins of "chat rooms." Remember the old chat rooms of the 1990s where you could go online and interact with people of similar interests? Many of us shied away from these, as they seemed to be a breeding ground for online lounge lizards. However, many diverse chat rooms still exist and continue to thrive today.

Chat rooms differ from Internet forums because in a chat room you "enter" a room (really a screen) and you see text as people type and interact directly in real time. One advantage of chat rooms is that you can receive real-time responses—it's like a group Instant Message. The cons? You need several people online at a time; there is no saved record of the conversation if you happen to forget what's been said; there's little overall structure; and you have to type pretty darn quickly to keep up or even hop into a conversation. Discussion boards require much less participation, and you can peruse them at your leisure.

2. Resource Boards

Many companies run resource boards as support for their products. These are especially common for technical services and products (such as iPods, web design software, or digital cameras), as sometimes members of the community (people who own the same product or service) can answer a question quicker than the company. In most cases, someone has asked your question before—that's the beauty of a resource board—and there is an online record of the question and answer for all to see. Many companies will direct you to their resource boards before you call customer service. This saves time for both you and the company. And, frankly, we love anything that helps us avoid the soul-killing experience of talking to an automated customer service phone line.

One caveat about resource boards: Because these boards are not always closely regulated, you might want to check out the people giving advice. If it's a company employee or someone who has a major presence on the board (it's a good sign when you can see multiple positive interactions with others on the board), you may be able to trust the information. However, if you ever are in doubt or your question is particularly complicated (e.g., it requires the use of a power tool), it's probably best to check directly with the company.

Savvy Tip #32: Resource boards are a great resource. If you want to know how to reset your BlackBerry™, just type "How do I reset my BlackBerry™?" into a search engine and, sure enough, several of the links that pop up will lead to a resource board. This also works for coupons and discounts if you're about to make a purchase. Just type in the product name and the word "coupon" or "discount" and you'll be directed to any special offers available.

3. Review Boards

Ushered in by the eBays and Amazons of the world, review boards are Internet forums that allow you to review products, services, retailers, professors, hotels, cars, etc. If you can see it, smell it, hear it, taste it or touch it, someone out there is running a review board that lets real people give real opinions about it. Why is this so popular? Because Generation X and Y have grown up distrusting traditional advertising. They know that it's pay-for-placement. If a magazine article is touting a particular cosmetic, they're apt to question whether that beauty editor received a complimentary year's supply or whether the company just bought a big whopping four-color ad.

Wendy's World, Wednesday, 11:55 a.m. *Check emails real quick before lunch. Alicia's book was just published. Brilliant! Will* *click on Amazon to see if it's there. Bingo. Do one-click shopping (rationalize that even if she gets a smaller royalty split than going to her publisher's site, it'll help her rankings). Make mental note to go back and write 5-star review. While I'm on here, where's that toy my nephews wanted? On sale! Great. But only two stars in the ratings? Scan the reviews. "This toy sux," from a six year old. "Didn't come with the special battery that costs more than the toy," says another. No wonder it's on sale. Guess I'll have to have a chat with the boys and find them something else. Maybe I could email BD guy? Now that we've resolved that the glamazon at lunch was his sister who has a son my nephews' age.*

Savvy Tip #33: Rank reviews. Yes, review boards can be set up with phony reviews and ratings, but that's why you need to look at the majority of the reviews. If everyone gives a certain computer a 7 or 8 out of 10, and one person gives it a 1 (bringing down the average ranking), you can assume that person either got a dud or works for a competitor. The beauty of online rankings is that unlike magazines, the public can weigh in with equal weight.

4. Announcement Boards

Internet forums are often used as classifieds, or announcement boards, where you can make announcements about items for sale, apartments for rent, events being held, tag sales, virtually anything. One of the most popular examples of this is Craig's List (www.craigslist.org). You can find just about anything on there, from roommates to jobs, to local classes and seminars.

Think of announcement boards as newspaper classified ads on steroids. Because most online announcement boards are free or low-cost, people can give a lot more information and even include photos—unlike newspaper classifieds where you pay for every character in the ad (hence, SWFs looking for SWMs and lxry apts w/hi clngs).

To demonstrate the diversity of what's available on such websites, we took a random click around Craigslist.org's local Austin, Texas, boards and found the following opportunities:

- Job posting for an Arabic linguist
- Downtown apartment available for rent during the Austin Film Festival
- Announcement of a missing grey tabby cat
- Offer of a rideshare to Houston
- Hot young male seeking a sizzling temptress (!)
- Feature film needing extras
- Ad for a camcorder repairman

Note that a website such as Craig's List also contains discussion forums. Because of the flexibility of the web, it's hard for any site to stick to one type of offering.

Listservs

What happens when you're too busy to visit your favorite resource board? Well, clearly this was why someone invented "listservs," which bring the boards right to your email. Officially, "LISTSERV®" is the trademark name for the first electronic mailing list software application, originally developed in 1986. The word "listserv" is now often used as a generic term for any email-based mailing list application. The standard generic terms are "electronic mailing list" or "email list," but most of the time you'll hear the term listserv.

A listserv is a communication tool that offers its members the opportunity to post suggestions or questions to a large number of people at the same time. When email is addressed to a listserv mailing list, it's automatically broadcast to everyone on the list (usually after being vetted by a list monitor). Each listserv targets pre-determined topics and discussions. For instance, you might join a "gardening buffs" listserv, or a member listserv for an association of which you're a member. If you're looking for listservs to join, check out Yahoo Groups (http://groups.yahoo.com), where you can search and join groups by topic.

The result of a listserv is similar to a newsgroup or forum, except that the messages are transmitted as email and are therefore available only to individuals on the list. The message appears just like a regular email message. The difference between a listserv and an e-newsletter is that an e-newsletter is sent from one person to many people. In a listserv, everyone on the list can use the system to send messages to everyone else on the list. But don't worry; you won't be bombarded with random emails. Listservs are set up so that you can select whether you want to be notified whenever something is posted, once a day, or once a week.

A Little Bit about "Lurking"

"Lurking," mentioned briefly above, is the term for reading online messages or online forum discussions without taking part in the discussion. Although the name makes this sound nefarious, it's generally considered a smart move. Go ahead and "lurk" in a particular discussion forum or listserv until you have some idea what the discussion is about and what the tone of the writers tends to be.

Some Internet forums and listservs are stricter than others. Before you post, check to see how other people post their messages. How specific are their post titles? (We think that the more specific, the better. "Seeking college student intern for fashion magazine" is better than "Seeking intern.") Check out all the boards before posting as well, so you can find the right category for your post. We've heard about a Red Sox fan blog where you will get berated for posting general comments on the "Game Threads" board. So, avoid the berating by doing a little pre-post lurking.

Savvy Tip #34: The final, most important online networking tip to remember: Always peruse before you post. Each different platform, whether it's a message board, blog, listserv, or social network has its own unwritten rules (although often on message boards, they're even written down). Spend some time seeing how others operate, and you'll be able to blend right in!

Conclusion: From Victorian to Virtual...Here Ends Our Tale

And so we come to the end of our discussion of online networking. As you have seen, the opportunities to build and maintain contacts through the web are virtually (pun intended!) limitless. Your success is only limited by the number of emails you send, the number of posts on your blog, the number of connections on your social networking profile, and the amount of time you can type without developing carpal tunnel syndrome.

However…

We cannot sign off without reminding you one last time that online networking must be carried out in addition to—not instead of—in-person networking. No matter how brilliant an online networker you are (and we know you are an expert now!), nothing beats the sense and sensibility of human contact.

> ***Wendy's World, Thursday, 9:07 p.m.*** *Well, it's off to reunion in a few weeks, and get this: BD guy, who has now been elevated to BF (yes, a boyfriend), has made an actual commitment a whole month in advance to accompany me and provide what I'm sure will be well-needed comic relief. Perhaps that will keep me from tossing my cookies when I see that loser Chris Martin (or his poor wife).*
>
> *But, back to the BF. Got to hand it to a guy who will not only escort a gal to her reunion, but will also help with her job hunt. (Note to self: Follow up with C and the gals about the new career game plan. Perhaps we'll schedule an evening out to brainstorm about possibilities? It's amazing how many more connections we can come up with over a cocktail.)*
>
> *BF also gets extra points for keeping me entertained with a steady flow of cute emails while I'm exiled here in Delaware at a client site. So they're not romantic letters of Jane Austen's day, but they're romantic in today's sense (a man who sends me job leads!).*

Not only that, he's promised to read a Jane Austen novel if I read one by his favorite, Carl Hiaasen. I'm only halfway through his pick for me so far, and I hate to admit it, this English major is totally digging Hiaasen, and the South Floridian wackos he writes about. In fact, I think it's time to take a reading break...TTFN![32].

CLICK ... LOG OFF ... SHUT DOWN.

---

[32] Ta Ta For Now!

Appendix I: The Story behind the Downtown Women's Club

By Diane K. Danielson, CEO and Founder, Downtown Women's Club

Throughout this book, we make mention of the Downtown Women's Club (DWC), as many members contributed their expertise and participated in our survey about online networking. Now we'd like to share with you a bit more about the DWC and why it's such a unique organization. We also hope that you'll visit our website at www.downtownwomensclub.com and start putting your savvy new online networking skills to work ASAP!

What is the Downtown Women's Club?

The Downtown Women's Club is an online and in-person business network for women. We currently have 13 member-launched, customized local chapters in Atlanta, Boston, Chicago, Detroit, Los Angeles, NYC, Pittsburgh, Phoenix, Providence, San Diego, San Francisco, Washington, DC, and Worcester, MA. We hope to add more cities and markets in the future (see Appendix II for more information about how to start a local DWC chapter). Our website, DowntownWomensClub.com, includes the DWC Plus member directory, a proprietary, Internet-searchable member directory for career women, teleclasses that you can download on demand, and a number of ways for our members to share information and promote their businesses and their careers to each other and the world.

Why did I found the Downtown Women's Club?

The Downtown Women's Club began in 1998 as an effort to make networking fun and accessible to women. It was also a great excuse to get together with other savvy, professionally passionate gals. Over the past few years, we've been expanding the DWC platform both geographically and virtually because my particular passion is helping women shatter glass ceilings, leap over gender gaps in a single bound, and generally shake up the corporate landscape.

I truly believe technology is one of the keys to leveling the playing field and that's why we've spent the past few years creating online opportunities for our members. Women can participate in DWC in-person or online no matter where they work, live, or play—from 9-to-5 or at 2 a.m. Many of our members don't even have a local chapter in their area and that's why our motto is *"Downtown Women: it's an attitude, not a location."*

Our goal at the DWC is to help women gain the business experience, contacts, skills, and information they need to compete … as well as to have some serious fun! Our vision for the DWC is to create a social and professional community for corporate executives, entrepreneurs, and anyone moving in and out of the job market with or without family demands. We want to provide the help, support, and community we all need in a way that is convenient and effective for everyone involved.

What's unique about the DWC?

1. **Clicks and mix networking**. The DWC is one of the few women's organizations to successfully combine online and in-person networking. We understand that busy professional women are trying to do it all (because we're trying to do it all, too!). So, we've invested heavily in maintaining our low-key, low-cost, high-impact local chapters, while at the same time developing more virtual services like our member directory, our DWC LinkedIn.com and Facebook.com groups, message boards, teleclasses, and a variety of different ways for our members to market their businesses online.

2. **Personal and professional development**. We know from our own experience that if networking isn't fun, then women just aren't going to bother doing it! We want to make sure our members are motivated to network, but not at the expense of their personal lives. This is why we provide almost as many "fun" events—like salon or

shopping nights, teleclasses about online dating, and book reviews of beach read novels—as we do professionally-focused services. So grab some girlfriends (or come meet some new ones) and join in on the fun.

3. **Cross-industry networks.** When we began the DWC nearly a decade ago, we realized that to be successful professionals, we needed contacts both within our industry and in the community at large. This is why you'll find executives from all industries as well as entrepreneurial members. While many of our programs are useful to all our members, you will often see a few geared to specific needs ('cause everyone needs a little special attention sometimes.)

4. **Corporate women's initiative support**. Running a women's initiative program at a company can be difficult, but it's rewarding for both the employees and the company. We would love to see more of these, and this is why we've created a corporate sponsorship program where we can provide resources to your own in-house network, including employee retention *and* recruiting programs. Even if your company is too small to support your own in-house network, we have corporate memberships available so you can purchase memberships for your employees at a discounted rate.

5. **Low-key, low-cost networking**. We're not as formal as most organizations, and we depend on our members to keep our local clubs running and to spread the word about DWC. Yet, we've found that by avoiding formalities, our members take charge and get more out of the DWC community. We hope to keep our in-person clubs low-key and low-cost, but this is dependent upon sponsors and members stepping up to become DWC Plus subscribers (at only $49.99/year, it's no more than the cost of one venti, half-caf, vanilla soy latte per month, and DWC is 100% fat and cholesterol free).

6. **No guilt networking**. We've heard over and over about how women are tired of paying significant dues to networking organizations and then not being able to fit them into their busy schedules. We also realize that women today have a tough time committing to a sit-down lunch or dinner and get tired of hearing the same speakers at every organization. This is why we have smaller, more casual events often featuring some of our members or new speakers we've discovered. Still can't fit events into your schedule? That's why we developed our DWC Plus online networking platform, so that our members can interact in a comfortable environment whether it's in-person or online.

7. **Our "business is fun" philosophy**. From the very beginning, the DWC has attracted women who like their careers and want to prosper, but they also want to have some fun along the way. This is why we try to include an element of fun in everything we do, whether it's our blogs, our teleclasses, or our local networking events.

Is there really still a need for women's groups?

I often get asked whether, in this day and age, there's still a need for women's business networks. My answer is always the same: Yes! And that's not just because the DWC business plan is based on it. Until women make up a respectable number on the Fortune 500 CEO list, or the media stops creating "mommy wars" and "opting-out" guilt trips where there shouldn't be any, then, yes, women need the support of other women and access to information, networks and platforms that they may not be getting in their own companies.

For more about the Downtown Women's Club, visit our website at www.downtownwomensclub.com or our "Women's DISH" blog at www.womensDISH.com.

Diane K. Danielson
CEO and Founder, Downtown Women's Club

Appendix II: Start Your Own Downtown Women's Club Local Chapter

At the Downtown Women's Club, we promote networking as something that should be low-cost, fun, and convenient. That's why we keep the process for starting and running local chapters as simple as possible. We call the process DWC-123 and it really follows our grassroots philosophy. Here's how it works:

1. **Grab your girlfriends, as well as your colleagues, clients, former classmates, and neighbors.** Wherever you look, there are businesswomen just like you who understand the need to network and want to do so in a fun and welcoming environment. All you need is a handful of dynamic, energetic women willing to try something new. We recommend a group of about six women to start. Find others by submitting event announcements to local online and off-line event calendars, such as newspapers or your local Craig's List.

2. **Designate a director (or two).** One person (or even two) must assume the club's "director" role. Without someone being ultimately responsible and "in charge," any club will fail. The responsibilities of the director include arranging the events and sending out announcements (via email). We highly recommend having a program committee to help plan events, fill in for the director(s) when necessary, and spread the word about your club. Directors are usually well-connected women (or those who plan to be well-connected women) who are or will be leaders in their community. Our most successful directors are women who thrive on expanding their own network but are also dedicated to supporting other women in business.

3. **Plan some get-togethers.** In start-up mode, local clubs usually hold monthly brownbag lunches, coffees, or cocktails (pick the one that works for you). Once the first event is set, send out email

invitations to everyone you think might be interested—colleagues, clients, and friends. You can use a free service like Evite.com or Meetup.com, create a Yahoo or Google group, or simply keep an email list. First meetings tend to be "get to know you" events. After that, it helps to invite facilitators or speakers on professional development topics. But don't feel the need to be too stuffy. Programs like "Fashion and Finance" and "Feng Shui Your Office" have been big hits! Grow your membership by encouraging attendees to bring one or two new people each month and to pass along the information to their clients, colleagues, and friends. You can also post announcements in free local event listing spots like Craig's List and your local newspaper or business journal.

Sound easy? Well, it is really that easy. The following are the only technical steps you need to know to get up and running. Note: you don't have to contact DWC National if you follow these guidelines.

1. Make sure there are no sanctioned local clubs in your area by checking our "Clubs and Calendars" section of the DowntownWomensClub.com website. The clubs listed on our site are our sanctioned local clubs—they have homepages and calendars, and DWC National handles the distribution of their calendar announcements to members.

2. Make sure there are no unsanctioned local clubs in your area by checking our DWC-123 Start-Up Club Board (also called DWC Chat on our website). Under the DWC-123 Start-Up Club Board will be any new clubs that women, like you, are starting around the country. Generally, we like our clubs to be about 50 miles away from each other. If someone has posted an interest in starting one in your area, then join forces!

3. If there are no local clubs in your area, go to the DWC-123 Start-Up Club Board and post the name of your region "DWC-[your city, town, or metro area], followed by the state" in the forum header. Then, in the content, post your contact information and encourage

people who are interested in helping get this off the ground to contact you.

Sample posting:

Header: DWC-Las Vegas, NV

Hi! I'm a new transplant to LV and wanted to meet other ambitious and fun businesswomen. If you'd like to help me launch the DWC-LV, please contact me:

Ima Coolchick
ImaCoolchick@gmail.com

4. After posting your announcements, you should then call a meeting with any and all interested individuals—these are your likely prospects for your program committee. You can post this meeting on the DWC-123 Start-Up Club Board, or wait until after your planning meeting to post info about an official public meeting.

   Sample posting:

   Header: DWC-Las Vegas, NV Kickoff Meeting – Jan. 6th

   We're kicking off the DWC-LV on January 6th with cocktails from 6:00–8:00 p.m. at the Hard Rock Café. Come join us to brainstorm and network. Please RSVP (although we won't necessarily hold you to it!), so that we have your email address for future announcements.

   RSVP to: ImaCoolchick@gmail.com.

5. You can build the club by email by keeping a master list or using a free program like Yahoo Groups. Some clubs don't require RSVPs for events like cocktails at a local bar or restaurant where it's pay as you go and there is no special reserved room. For lunches or

workshops at corporate locations, it's best to require RSVPs either for building security purposes or room size.

6. Use the DWC-123 Start-Up Club Board to post your future meetings, so that new members can find you. (But don't depend on that to drive people there; you also need to get the word out locally through free online event listings in your area.) Members can also use the board to make suggestions and ask questions. Note that DWC National does not monitor these boards or our unsanctioned local clubs in any manner.

7. Your club can apply to be sanctioned by DWC National when you hit the landmark of six consecutive months of meetings AND have a distribution list of 100+ members. At that time, contact help@downtownwomensclub.com. We'll then get you up on our calendars and create a personalized email template for you.

8. If you achieve sanctioned status, then DWC National will take over the distribution and communications to members and your local club will get a homepage and calendar. Your only responsibilities after that will be to plan programs and update your online calendar.

How about that? You can start an organization from scratch without a whole lot of bureaucracy!

What if you already have a women's network that meets in person, but you don't have much of an online presence? Apply for your network to become a Downtown Women's Club affiliate chapter and your members can take advantage of our online programs, and you can continue to run the club locally, exactly as you always have.

We look forward to expanding our Downtown Women's Club community and seeing more of your fabulous faces on our website!

Appendix III: Six Commandments for Running a Local Chapter

A few years ago, we were asked to create guidelines for running a local Downtown Women's Club (DWC) chapter. Because we believe that each chapter and every director is unique, we came up with six principles (or commandments, as we like to call them). We'll leave the details up to you.

6. **Membership and events are open to everyone**. This means everyone, including men! While our platform tends to be self-selecting for most members, our DWC local clubs and events are and will remain open to everyone. No local club shall discriminate against any individual for any reason.

5. **Local club events are open to all people, members or not.** We're always asked "How do you do this so low cost?" In order to continue the convenience of low-cost, low-commitment in-person clubs, we have launched some paid online services like DWC Plus which help to subsidize the clubs along with corporate sponsors and advertising opportunities. While we may have some more expensive events along the way (with discounts to DWC Plus members), we want to ensure that networking at the DWC stays accessible to everyone.

   We hope that directors will recommend that your local members join as DWC Plus members, so that we can keep operating in this fashion and so that our in-person members will feel like they are getting a lot more out of the Downtown Women's Club experience.

   Even more reason not to charge large amounts at in-person events is the fact that when people pay to network, they expect networking to happen to them. Yet when it's low-cost, they tend to be more proactive and collaborative! This is what makes the DWC so unique and welcoming.

4. **Events can be small/interactive**. Apply the "what's in it for me?" test. Women today are too busy to make it to an event where there is no immediate gratification. We've found that smaller (10-75 women) events just seem to work better. Also, we have the most success with speakers who engage attendees in interactive discussions and who will leave our members with information they can apply immediately to further their professional and personal development.

3. **Topics can be professional/personal mix.** Keep things lively by mixing it up. We are a professional women's organization, yet we've found that our members enjoy programs that mix the personal development with the professional. For example, fashion and finance; book clubs and cocktails; shopping and networking, etc. Feel free to step outside the "corporate" mindset once in a while and have some serious fun!

2. **Be wary of blatant self-marketing.** This backfires for both directors and members. We know it's tempting, but we strongly recommend fighting the urge to blanket members with solicitations. Members are entrusting directors with their email addresses. If you use them inappropriately, you will lose the trust and interest of your membership and damage your own reputation. Please stick to DWC business in your emails (although your signature and tagline can definitely be attached at the end), and we STRONGLY recommend using the "BCC" box whenever you forward any emails to your group.

1. **Don't forget to have fun!** One of the reasons we keep everything so simple and with minimal bureaucracy is that if it isn't fun, we wouldn't keep doing it. So, if you're starting a club, don't ever forget the "fun factor" for both club organizers and members.

For more about starting and running a Downtown Women's Club local chapter, please visit www.downtownwomensclub.com.

About the Authors

Diane K. Danielson (left) is the CEO and founder of the Downtown Women's Club (www.DowntownWomensClub.com), a professional network and career website for businesswomen. She is also the co-author of *Table Talk: The Savvy Girl's Alternative to Networking* (2003), a contributing writer to *PINK* magazine, and a blogger for the *Boston Globe* and *Entrepreneur* magazine. When not writing, she runs workshops and speaks at corporations, associations, and universities around the country. More of her random musings and career tips can be found on her blog at www.womensDISH.com. *Author photo by Melissa Forman.*

Lindsey Pollak (right) is a columnist and blogger for the Downtown Women's Club. She is the author of *Getting from College to Career: 90 Things to Do Before You Join the Real World* (HarperCollins, 2007) and has written for *Marie Claire* magazine, *PINK* magazine and *New York Metro* newspaper. Lindsey is also a frequent speaker at corporations, associations and universities around the country. For more information and a link to her blog, visit www.lindseypollak.com. *Author photo by Emily Travis.*

Printed in the United States
112192LV00002B/1-213/P

9 781601 452535